STUDENT U

AS Chemistry
UNIT 3

AQA

Module 3: Introduction to Organic Chemistry/Practical

Neil Goldie

Philip Allan Updates
Market Place
Deddington
Oxfordshire
OX15 0SE

tel: 01869 338652
fax: 01869 337590
e-mail: sales@philipallan.co.uk
www.philipallan.co.uk

ISBN 0 86003 744 4

This Guide has been written specifically to support students preparing for the AQA AS Chemistry Unit 3 examination. The content has been neither approved nor endorsed by AQA and remains the sole responsibility of the author.

Printed by Information Press, Eynsham, Oxford

P00068

Update September 2002

STUDENT UNIT GUIDES

UNITS 1, 2 & 3

AS Chemistry

AQA

Module 1: Atomic Structure, Bonding and Periodicity

Module 2: Foundation Physical and Inorganic Chemistry

Module 3: Introduction to Organic Chemistry/Practical

Changes to the AS assessment from summer 2003

The duration of the written papers for Units 1, 2 and 3 will be reduced to **1 hour**. The papers will have the current style and format but the raw mark total for each paper will be 60. They will all be timetabled together.

The format of the practical exam has not changed. It will be timetabled separately outside the main timetable period. Students carrying out the practical coursework need only submit one mark score per skill area to cover the minimum requirement, but they must come from at least two different modules.

The author

PA/089 PA/100 PA/034

Contents

Introduction

About this guide

This guide is for students following the AQA Chemistry AS specification. It deals with Unit 3, which examines the content of **Module 3(a): Introduction to Organic Chemistry** and **Module 3(b): Practical Work**. Unit 3(a) covers 25% of the total AS marks, or $12\frac{1}{2}$% of the total A-level marks. The exam consists of several structured questions, of varying length, which are all compulsory. Some questions require short answers while some are more extended, needing answers written in continuous prose. Unit 3(b) assesses 15% of the total AS marks or $7\frac{1}{2}$% of the total A-level marks. This section is assessed either by coursework carried out throughout the year or by a practical exam.

The key to success

It is essential that you can recall the basic facts and definitions, but a deeper understanding of the subject is essential if you want to achieve the top grades. The key to success in chemistry is *to understand the fundamental concepts* and *be able to apply them to new and unfamiliar situations*. Good examination technique is also an important factor, enabling you to work more effectively in the exam and gain access to the marks needed for a top grade.

This guide allows you to look again at the content of the specification, to test yourself at the end of each section and to assess your own work. It is essential that you read through the examiner's comments because they will help you improve your exam technique. Once you have completely worked through this guide, you will be very aware of your weak areas and it is these areas that you really need to address. Make a list of these weak areas and discuss any problems with other students in your class and with your teacher.

Using this guide

This guide has three sections:

- **Introduction** — this provides guidance on study and revision, together with advice on approaches and techniques to ensure you answer the examination questions in the best way that you can.
- **Content Guidance** — this section is not intended to be a textbook. It offers guidelines on the main features of the content of Unit 3, together with particular advice on making study more productive.
- **Questions and Answers** — this shows you the sort of questions you can expect in the unit test. Grade-A answers are provided; these are followed by examiner's comments. Careful consideration of these will improve your answers and, much more importantly, will improve your understanding of the chemistry involved.

Revise a topic using the Content Guidance section as a guide. If there is something you do not understand, you should also refer to your own class notes and textbooks.

Try to be specific when asking teachers questions. For instance, 'Please could you explain haloalkanes again' will not lead to good use of your time if you understand most of the features. 'Please could you explain concurrent displacement and elimination, particularly the mechanisms' is more specific and shows that you have worked hard to identify weak areas.

Once you have revised a particular topic thoroughly, you should attempt the relevant question in the Question and Answer section, *without* looking at the grade-A answer.

Compare your answer with the grade-A answer and estimate your own performance. A rough guide to use is 80% = grade A, 70% = grade B, 60% = grade C, etc. However, these grade boundaries are adjusted, depending on the performance of the candidates.

Read through the examiner's comments to find out if you have made any of the common mistakes and to see how you could improve your technique. The comments also give some alternative answers.

Make a note of *specific questions* that caused you problems and discuss them with other students and your teacher.

Revision schedule

- Plan your revision schedule carefully.
- It is essential that you revise regularly.
- Leave yourself enough time to cover all the material. You need to go through each topic once as a basic minimum and then go through the weak areas again.
- In the weeks leading up to the exam, it is the weak areas that you should be revising, not every topic.
- In each revision session, do not try to achieve too much. Revise one topic per session, e.g. nomenclature and isomerism. Here is one way to structure your session:
  - revise from the Content Guidance section (and your own notes)
  - make a brief written summary (no more than an A4 sheet of paper)
  - attempt the question
  - mark your answer
  - read the examiner's comments
- If you have scored a grade A, then tick the topic in the table shown below. You must have a break before you start the revision of the next topic.
- If there are weak areas and questions that you clearly do not understand, then write down specific questions ready for discussion with your teacher.

- Finally, make sure that you attempt all the past paper questions from the exam board and study the mark schemes carefully. Questions may be repeated or similar questions set.

Revision checklist

Once you have completed your revision and you feel that you understand the topic fully, tick the relevant box. If you have identified a weak area, place a cross in the relevant box.

Nomenclature and isomerism

Topics	Details	✓ or ✗
Nomenclature	• Empirical formula, molecular and structural formulae • Homologous series and functional groups • Naming of simple organic compounds, limited to chains with up to 6 carbon atoms	
Isomerism	• Structural isomerism • Chain, position and functional group isomerism • Geometrical isomerism in alkenes	

Petroleum and alkanes

Topics	Details	✓ or ✗
Fractional distillation	• Petroleum is a mixture of mainly alkane hydrocarbons • Separation of the fractions because of their different boiling points • Major fractions and their uses	
Cracking	• Cracking involves the breaking of a C–C bond • Thermal cracking occurs by a free-radical mechanism at high pressure and high temperature, producing a high percentage of alkenes • Catalytic cracking occurs by a carbocation mechanism at slight pressure and high temperature in the presence of a zeolite catalyst; it is used mainly to produce motor fuels and aromatic hydrocarbons • Economic reasons for cracking of alkanes (e.g. production of ethene for poly(ethene) and the conversion of heavy fractions into higher-value products)	
Combustion	• Combustion of the sulphur impurities in petroleum produces oxides of sulphur, which are toxic and cause acid rain • Complete and incomplete combustion and the origin of the pollutants NO_x, CO and unburned hydrocarbons • Removal of pollutants by catalytic converters	
Chlorination of alkanes	• Reaction mechanism of methane with chlorine as a free-radical substitution reaction in terms of initiation, propagation and termination	

Alkenes

Topics	Details	✓ or ✗
Structure and bonding	• Bonding in alkenes involves a double covalent bond • The planar nature of C=C • The double bond is a centre of high electron density	
Reactions	• Hydrogenation and its use in the manufacture of margarine • Decolourisation of bromine water as a test for alkenes • Mechanism of electrophilic addition with HBr, H_2SO_4 and Br_2 • Electrophilic addition to unsymmetrical alkenes by reference to the relative stabilities of carbocation intermediates • Hydration of alkenes in the presence of an acid catalyst • Industrial production of ethanol from ethene • Formation of addition polymers from alkenes	
Epoxyethane	• Production of epoxyethane from ethene and oxygen in the presence of a silver catalyst, including the hazards of the process • Epoxyethane is a three-membered ring under strain, so it is highly reactive • Hydrolysis of epoxyethane produces diols, which are important in the production of antifreeze and polyesters • Reactions of epoxyethane and alcohols give products that are used in the preparation of solvents, plasticisers and surfactants	

Haloalkanes

Topics	Details	✓ or ✗
Nucleophilic substitution	• Haloalkanes contain polar bonds • Haloalkanes are susceptible to nucleophilic attack, limited to OH^-, CN^- and NH_3 • Mechanism of nucleophilic substitution in primary haloalkanes • Influence of the carbon–halogen bond enthalpy on the rate of hydrolysis • Hydrolysis of nitriles to produce carboxylic acids	
Elimination	• Concurrent displacement and elimination (including mechanisms) in the reaction of a haloalkane with potassium hydroxide • Role of the OH^- ion as both a base and a nucleophile	

Alcohols

Topics	Details	✓ or ✗
Ethanol production	• Industrial production of ethanol by fermentation • Conditions for fermentation and the economic and environmental advantages and disadvantages of this process compared with industrial production from ethene	

Topics	Details	✓ or ✗
Classification and reactions	• The classification of alcohols as primary, secondary or tertiary • Use of potassium dichromate(VI) in the oxidation of alcohols • Oxidation of primary alcohols to aldehydes and carboxylic acids • Oxidation of secondary alcohols to ketones • Resistance of tertiary alcohols to oxidation • A chemical test to distinguish between aldehydes and ketones (e.g. Fehling's or Tollen's reagent) • Reduction of aldehydes to primary alcohols and ketones to secondary alcohols, using $NaBH_4$	
Elimination	• Dehydration of alcohols to form alkenes • Mechanism of elimination in terms of the loss of a proton from a carbocation generated from the protonated alcohol	

Unit Test 3(a)

If you have revised thoroughly, completed all the questions in this guide and discussed problems with other students and your teacher, you should enjoy the exam. If you have completed all the AQA past papers, then the style of the paper will be very familiar and you will recognise some questions in the exam because they will be similar to previous questions.

Do not begin to write as soon as you open the paper — quickly scan the questions first.

It is *not* essential that you answer the questions in order. If the first question is difficult, then leave it to the end. It *is* essential that you answer *all* the questions.

You will have enough time to answer all the questions, provided that you keep your answers concise and you do not include irrelevant information. It is easy to waste time writing out a section of your notes that is irrelevant to the question asked. Do not repeat the question when starting your answer. The key to exam success is achieving the maximum number of marks in the minimum number of words.

The mark allocation at the end of each question should be used to estimate the amount of detail needed in your answer. If there is 1 mark available, the examiner is looking for a key word or phrase and certainly no more than one sentence. If there are 4 marks available, you should include four key points, which usually means writing four short sentences.

No marks are available for producing neat answers, but it certainly helps the examiners when they are marking your work. Untidy diagrams may become inaccurate and this definitely loses marks.

Terms used in examination questions

Give/state/name

These appear in many of the early structured questions. You need only write one or two words. There is usually 1 mark available for questions of this type.

Define

It is essential that you learn all your definitions. You need to state a definition or law very concisely. Definitions are usually worth 2 or 3 marks and the mark allocation indicates how many key points must be included.

Complete

You have to finish off a diagram, a graph or a table.

Draw the structure

When drawing the structures of organic compounds it is essential that each carbon atom is surrounded by four bonds. You must include all the hydrogen atoms in the structure.

Write, draw or outline a mechanism

Drawing the mechanism of an organic reaction means showing how the reactants interact to produce first an intermediate and then the final product. You must use curly arrows to represent the movement of electron pairs.

Calculate or determine

Use information to calculate a final answer that must be shown to the correct number of significant figures. Always show your working and include appropriate units after the final answer.

Write a balanced equation

In chemical equations, state symbols are not usually expected unless the examiner specifically asks for them. In organic reactions, it is important to show the structure of the reactants and the products rather than using molecular formulae.

Describe/explain

'Describe' means only give a description, whereas 'explain' requires a reason or interpretation. Both these terms mean more depth is required in your answer. You can judge how much detail is required by the mark allocation. 10 marks means that ten key points must be covered and this will probably require you to write a minimum of ten sentences. In general, most candidates write too much and give far too much detail.

Use

Questions using this term often include some data. Make sure you do use the data and include them in your answer. You may have to use a basic principle and apply it to a new and unfamiliar situation.

Suggest

This means that you will probably not have come across the material in the question before. You will have been taught the basic principle and now you have to apply this knowledge to an unfamiliar situation. This is common in organic chemistry.

Content Guidance

This section covers the content of **Module 3(a): Introduction to Organic Chemistry**. The content of this module falls into five sections, which are summarised below.

Nomenclature and isomerism

Recall several definitions: empirical, molecular and structural formulae; homologous series and functional groups. Name simple organic compounds. Understand the concepts of structural isomerism (chain, position and functional group) and geometrical isomerism.

Petroleum and alkanes

Describe the separation of petroleum into fractions. Understand the principles of fractional distillation. Recall the names and uses of the fractions. Describe, with equations, the cracking of larger fractions into more useful smaller fractions and alkenes. Know the types of cracking (i.e. thermal and catalytic). Recall the different pollutants formed in the internal combustion engine; how they are formed, their effects on the environment and how they are removed by a catalytic converter. Describe the chlorination of alkanes with reference to the conditions, the equations and the free-radical mechanism.

Alkenes and epoxyethane

Describe the structure and bonding in alkenes. Understand the importance of the double bond in the chemistry of alkenes. Understand the mechanism and write equations for the electrophilic addition of alkenes with HBr, H_2SO_4 and Br_2. Predict the products of the addition to unsymmetrical alkenes by reference to the relative stabilities of the carbocation intermediates. Understand the industrial importance of alkenes, using hydrogenation, hydration and polymerisation as examples. Recall the equation and conditions for the industrial production of epoxyethane. Understand why epoxyethane is so reactive. Use equations to describe the reactions of epoxyethane with water and alcohols and state the uses of the products formed.

Haloalkanes

Understand the polar nature of haloalkanes and recall the equations, conditions and mechanisms for the nucleophilic substitution reactions involving OH^-, CN^- and NH_3. Predict the products of hydrolysis of nitriles. Understand how substitution and elimination can occur at the same time, particularly in secondary haloalkanes. Understand the role of the OH^- ion as both base and nucleophile in these reactions.

Alcohols

Compare and contrast the industrial production of ethanol via fermentation and hydration. Classify alcohols as primary, secondary or tertiary. Write equations and predict the structures of the products when alcohols are oxidised under different conditions. Write equations and predict the structures of the products when aldehydes and ketones are reduced to alcohols. Describe a simple chemical test to distinguish between aldehydes and ketones. Understand the mechanism and write equations for the elimination reaction in alkenes.

The section concludes with an overview of **Module 3(b): Practical Work**.

Nomenclature and isomerism

Definitions

- The **empirical formula** is the simplest whole number ratio of atoms of each element in a compound.
- The **molecular formula** is the actual number of atoms of each element in a compound.
- The **structural formula** shows the arrangement of the atoms and bonds within the molecule.
- A **functional group** is an atom or group of atoms that gives the organic compound its characteristic chemical properties.
- A **homologous series** is a family of organic compounds that possess the same general formula, show similar chemical properties and show a gradual change in physical properties. For example, the general formula of the alkanes is C_nH_{2n+2}; the general formula of the alkenes is C_nH_{2n}.

Naming organic compounds

Organic compounds are named according to the following rules:

- The root of the name is derived from the number of carbon atoms present in the longest **unbranched** chain:

Number of carbon atoms	1	2	3	4	5	6
Root	Meth-	Eth-	Prop-	But-	Pent-	Hex-

- If the carbon chain is joined up as a **ring**, then the prefix **cyclo**- is used.
- A chain can be **saturated** or **unsaturated** and this is indicated by the second syllable. If the chain is saturated (single bonds), the second syllable is '**-an-**', for example ethane, CH_3CH_3. If the chain is unsaturated (double bond), the second syllable is '**-en-**', for example ethene, $CH_2{=}CH_2$.
- A prefix or suffix is used to indicate the presence of a functional group. The suffix **-ol** indicates an alcohol, for example ethanol, CH_3CH_2OH. If no other functional group is present, then the name ends in the letter **e**.

CH_3CH_3	$CH_2{=}CH_2$	CH_3CH_2OH
Ethane	Ethene	Ethanol

- In many organic molecules, the carbon skeleton is **branched**. The names of the **side chains** depend on the number of carbon atoms in them: CH_3 is methyl; CH_3CH_2 is ethyl; $CH_3CH_2CH_2$ is propyl.

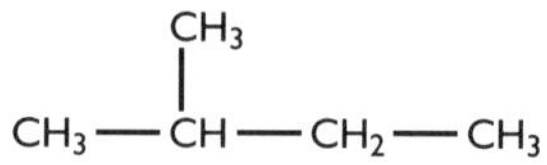

Methylbutane

- A *number* indicates the *position* of the functional group or side chain on the main carbon skeleton.

Propan-1-ol

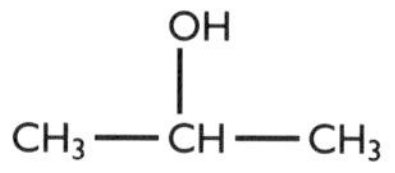

Propan-2-ol

- Carbon atoms are numbered consecutively from one end, such that the attached groups are on the *lowest numbered* carbon atoms.

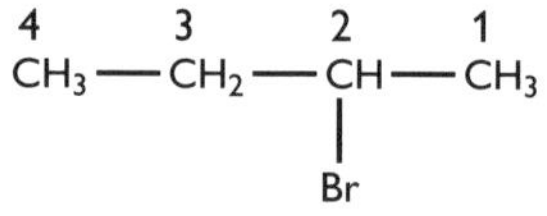

2-bromobutane

- To indicate the *position of a double bond*, the number of the lowest numbered carbon atom involved is placed before -ene, for example $CH_2{=}CHCH_2CH_3$ is called but-1-ene; $CH_3CH{=}CHCH_3$ is but-2-ene.
- **Aldehydes** (CHO), **acids** (COOH) and **nitriles** (CN) are always regarded as carbon number *one*.

CH_3CH_2CHO	CH_3CH_2COOH	CH_3CH_2CN
Propanal	Propanoic acid	Propanenitrile

- If the same functional group appears more than once, this is indicated by a prefix. **Di-** means *two* groups, **tri-** means *three* groups and **tetra-** means *four* groups.

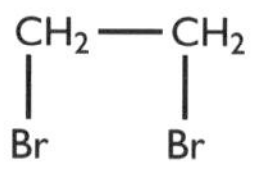

1,2-dibromoethane

- If more than one type of functional group is present, then positions and names are listed in alphabetical order of the functional group, i.e. bromo- before chloro- and tri**b**romo- before di**c**hloro-.

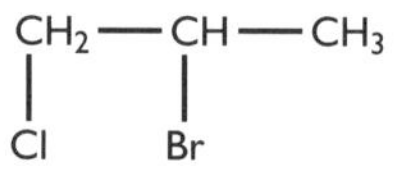

2-bromo-1-chloropropane

- When two names, which usually end in suffixes, are needed, the ending for **acid** takes precedence over **aldehyde** or **ketone**, which in turn takes precedence over **alcohol**.

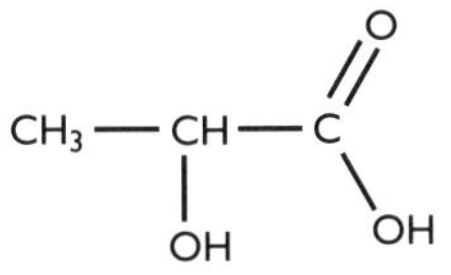

2-hydroxypropanoic acid

- The suffix **-en-** for alkenes can be placed in front of other suffixes to give, for example, **-enal** or **-enol**.

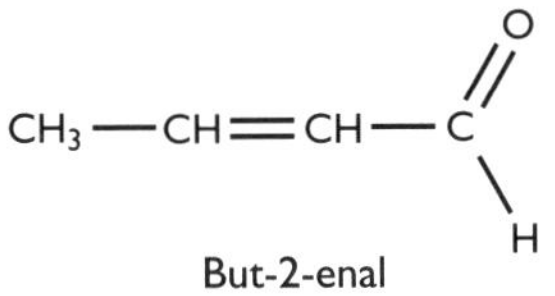

But-2-enal

Functional groups

In the table below, the functional groups are shown in bold in the examples.

Homologous series	Suffix/prefix	Examples with functional group shown in bold type
Alkanes	-ane	Butane $CH_3CH_2CH_2CH_3$ (no functional group)
Alkenes	-ene	But-2-ene $CH_3CH{=}CHCH_3$
Haloalkanes	Bromo- Chloro- Iodo-	1-chloropropane $CH_3CH_2CH_2\mathbf{Cl}$
Alcohols	-ol (or hydroxy-)	Propan-1-ol $CH_3CH_2CH_2\mathbf{OH}$
Aldehydes	-al	Ethanal 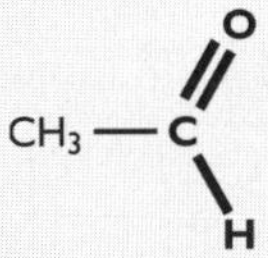
Ketones	-one	Butanone 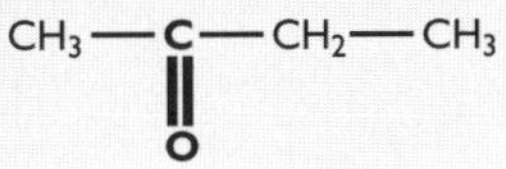

Homologous series	Suffix/prefix	Examples with functional group shown in bold type
Carboxylic acids	-oic acid	Propanoic acid 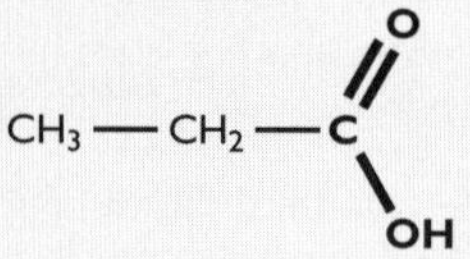
Amines	-amine	Ethylamine $CH_3CH_2\mathbf{NH_2}$
Amides	-amide	Propanamide 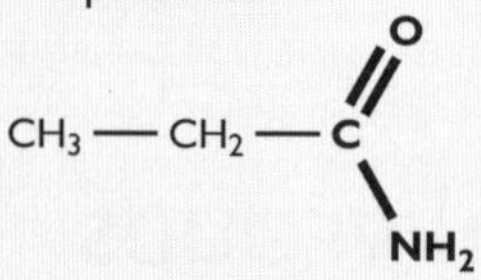
Nitriles	-nitrile	Butanenitrile $CH_3CH_2CH_2\mathbf{CN}$

Isomerism

The flow chart below shows the different types of isomerism.

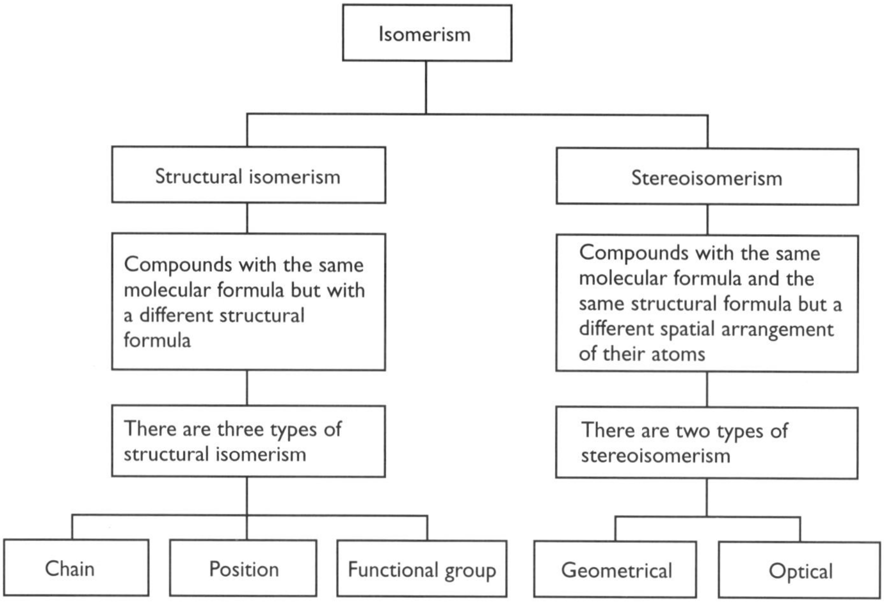

Chain isomerism

- This occurs when there are two or more ways of arranging the **carbon skeleton**.
- Chain isomers have similar chemical properties but slightly different physical properties.
- The more branched the isomer, the weaker are the van der Waals forces and the lower the boiling point.
- The isomers of C_5H_{12} are examples of chain isomerism.

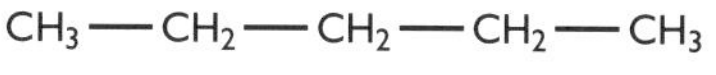

Pentane

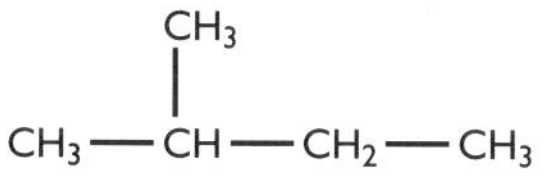

Methylbutane

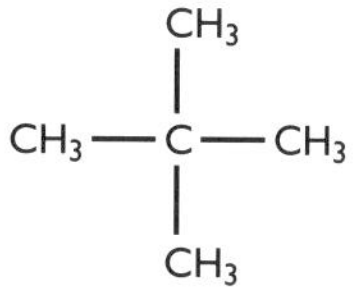

Dimethylpropane (lowest boiling point)

Position isomerism

- These isomers have the same carbon skeleton and the same functional group.
- The functional group is joined at *different* places on the carbon skeleton.
- The isomers of C_3H_7Br are examples of position isomerism.

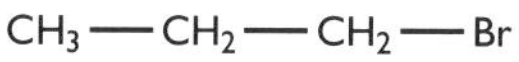

1-bromopropane

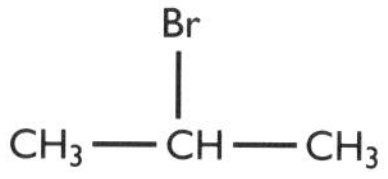

2-bromopropane

Functional group isomerism

- These isomers have different functional groups.
- They have different chemical properties.
- They have different physical properties.
- The isomers of C_3H_6O are examples of functional group isomerism.

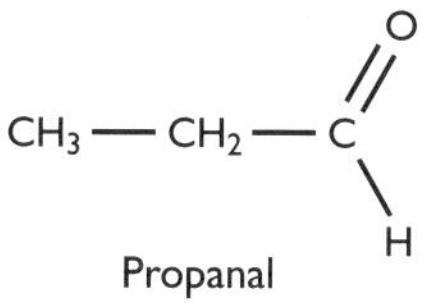

Propanal

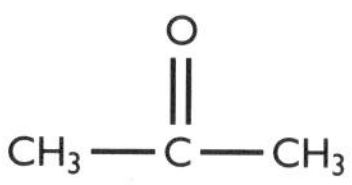

Propanone

Geometrical isomerism

- Geometrical isomerism is also known as ***cis–trans*** isomerism.
- It is caused by **the non-rotation of the double bond** in alkenes.
- It is not possible to have geometrical isomers when there are two identical groups joined to the same carbon in a double bond.
- 1,2-dichloroethene exhibits geometrical isomerism.

cis

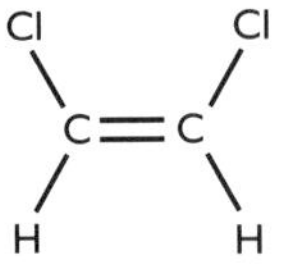

trans

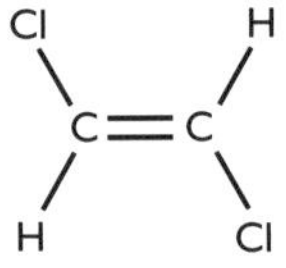

- 1,1-dichloroethene does not show geometrical isomerism.

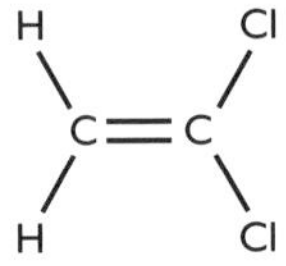

A common question requires you to draw and name the three isomeric alkenes of molecular formula C_4H_8 and to indicate which one is capable of exhibiting geometrical isomerism.

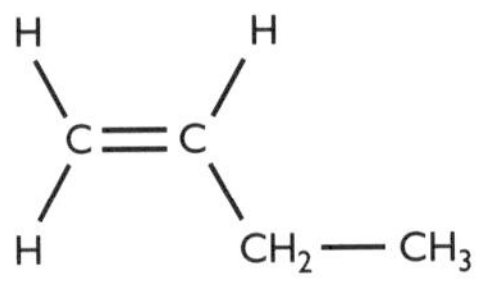

But-1-ene

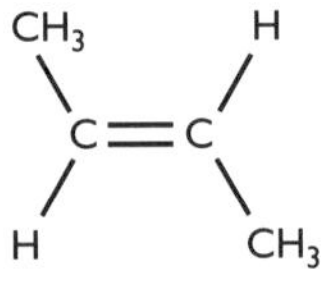

But-2-ene

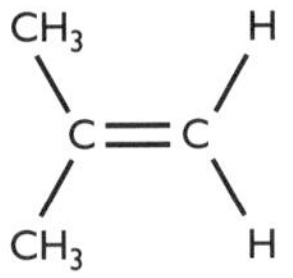

Methylpropene

Only this isomer is capable of showing geometrical isomerism; the one shown is the *trans* isomer and the other will be the *cis* isomer

The other type of stereoisomerism is optical isomerism. This is covered in Module 4.

Petroleum and alkanes

You need to know the components of crude oil, how the different fractions are separated and at least one use of each fraction.

You need to understand the principle of cracking and know that different types of cracking are used to produce different products for the petrochemical industry.

The chemistry of alkanes is limited because of their unreactive nature. The emphasis in this section is on their combustion and chlorination. Many candidates find the mechanism of chlorination and the equations for cracking the most difficult.

Crude oil and fractional distillation

Crude oil is:

- a dark, viscous liquid

- a mixture of many different hydrocarbons (mainly alkanes) with a trace of sulphur compounds
- formed by decomposition, under intense heat and pressure, of marine and plant life over millions of years

The separation of crude oil

The method used to separate crude oil is **fractional distillation**:

- Crude oil is separated into a number of simpler mixtures (**fractions**), which are useful as fuels, lubricants and as a source of petrochemicals.
- The fractions contain different molecules which have **different boiling point ranges**.
- The crude oil is vaporised and passed into a tall fractionating column.
- A **temperature gradient** exists in the column, which is hot at the bottom and cooler at the top.
- The fractions cool and condense at different levels — the smaller the molecule, the weaker are the van der Waals forces between the molecules, the greater is its volatility and the higher in the column it condenses.
- The crude oil residue is distilled further under vacuum. Lowering the pressure reduces the boiling point and ensures the constituents distil off below their decomposition temperature (i.e. it avoids cracking).

The simplified diagram below shows all that you need to know about the fractional distillation process. You need to be able to *name all the fractions* and *give one use of each fraction*. In addition, you need to understand the principle that small molecules with weak intermolecular forces are found at the top of the fractionating column, where it is cooler.

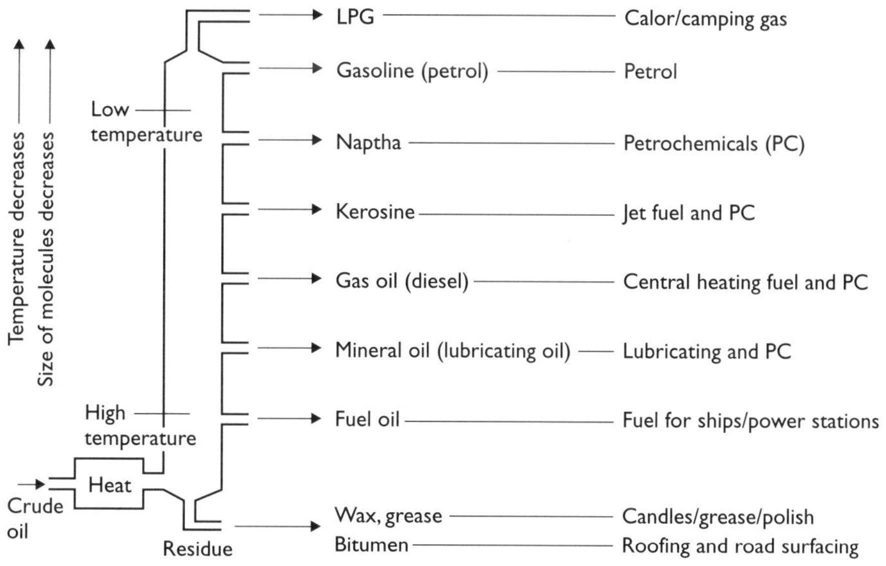

The demand for the fractions is not uniform. Demand for fractions containing alkanes of low M_r exceeds supply. The supply of fractions containing alkanes of high M_r exceeds demand. Alkanes of large M_r are broken down (**cracked**) to produce smaller-chain alkanes (more useful as fuels) and alkenes (which can be used to produce polymers and other chemicals).

The cracking of alkanes

Cracking is the breaking of large alkanes into smaller molecules.

$$\text{Large } M_r \text{ alkane} \xrightarrow{\text{heat}} \text{Smaller } M_r \text{ alkane} + \text{alkene (or hydrogen)}$$

- Cracking can resolve the imbalance in the supply and demand of the fractions.
- Many of the smaller molecules are more useful as fuels such as petrol.
- Small, unsaturated molecules such as ethene and propene are also produced. These alkenes are used to make polymers and other chemicals.
- High temperatures required for cracking cause C–C and C–H bonds to break, producing smaller molecules and alkenes.
- In addition, other processes take place, such as **dehydrogenation** (loss of hydrogen to convert alkanes to alkenes and cycloalkanes to aromatic compounds), **cyclisation** (converting straight chains to cyclic compounds) and **isomerisation** (converting straight-chain alkanes to branched alkanes).
- The long-chain molecules can break up in many different ways to produce a mixture of products, which can be separated by fractional distillation.

You may be asked to construct a number of different equations to describe the process of cracking. The examiner will give you all the information you need in the question. Remember that the original, large molecule cracked will be an alkane, which breaks down to give a shorter-chain alkane and an unsaturated alkene. Always remember to check that the numbers of carbon atoms and hydrogen atoms on each side of the equation are exactly the same.

The following equations show the cracking of a long-chain alkane with 14 carbon atoms.

$$C_{14}H_{30} \rightarrow C_7H_{16} + C_3H_6 + 2C_2H_4$$
$$C_{14}H_{30} \rightarrow C_{12}H_{24} + C_2H_4 + H_2$$
$$C_{14}H_{30} \rightarrow C_8H_{18} + C_6H_{12}$$

The equations you write will depend on the information given by the examiner.

Types of cracking

The type of cracking and the proportions of final products from the cracking process depend upon the conditions employed.

Thermal cracking

- High temperatures (800–900 °C) and high pressures are used.
- A high proportion of alkenes is produced.
- The higher temperature causes the chains to break near their ends, producing small alkenes such as ethene.
- The C–C bonds break via **homolytic bond fission**.
- The intermediates produced are **free radicals**.

Catalytic cracking

- Lower temperatures (450 °C) and only a slight pressure are used.
- **Zeolite catalysts** — crystalline **aluminosilicates** — are required.
- Branched alkanes, cycloalkanes and aromatic hydrocarbons are produced.
- Branched alkanes burn more uniformly and so are more useful as motor fuels.
- The intermediates produced are **carbocations**.

The combustion of hydrocarbons

Hydrocarbons produce a variety of products on combustion. Limited (incomplete) combustion of hydrocarbons produces **carbon** or **carbon monoxide** and water. Complete combustion of hydrocarbons produces **carbon dioxide** and **water**. The three equations for methane are shown below:

$$CH_4 + O_2 \longrightarrow C + 2H_2O$$
$$CH_4 + 1\tfrac{1}{2}O_2 \longrightarrow CO + 2H_2O$$
$$CH_4 + 2O_2 \longrightarrow CO_2 + 2H_2O$$

The examiner could ask you to balance equations for the combustion of any hydrocarbon, with the most popular choice being equations for hydrocarbons such as C_8H_{18}.

Pollutants and the internal combustion engine

- Incomplete combustion of C_8H_{18} produces carbon monoxide:
  $$C_8H_{18} + 8\tfrac{1}{2}O_2 \longrightarrow 8CO + 9H_2O$$
- The reaction of N_2 and O_2 (present in air) via the spark in the engine produces **nitrogen monoxide**:
  $$N_2 + O_2 \longrightarrow 2NO$$

These pollutants cause problems because:

- carbon monoxide is **toxic**
- nitrogen monoxide is oxidised to nitrogen dioxide, which dissolves in water to produce **acid rain**
- oxides of nitrogen (NO_x) react with unburnt hydrocarbons to produce **photochemical smog**

Removal of the pollutants by catalytic converters

- The gases are passed through a ceramic honeycomb structure coated in precious metals, such as **platinum**, **rhodium** and **palladium**.

- The ceramic support provides the maximum surface area, with minimal use of the metal to save costs.
- Carbon monoxide and nitrogen monoxide react to produce nitrogen and carbon dioxide, which are less harmful products:
  $CO + NO \longrightarrow CO_2 + \frac{1}{2}N_2$
- The unburnt hydrocarbons react with nitrogen monoxide to produce nitrogen, carbon dioxide and water:
  $C_8H_{18} + 25NO \longrightarrow 8CO_2 + 9H_2O + 12\frac{1}{2}N_2$

Chlorination of alkanes

Alkanes are **unreactive**, **saturated**, **non-polar** molecules with no electron-deficient or electron-rich sites. Therefore, they are not susceptible to attack by either nucleophiles (electron pair donors) or electrophiles (electron pair acceptors). However, alkanes do undergo **halogenation** reactions, as well as **combustion** and **cracking**.

When methane and chlorine are mixed together in the dark, no reaction occurs. When the mixture is exposed to UV light, a mixture of substituted chloroalkanes is produced due to a photochemical reaction.

- **Equation for monosubstitution:** $CH_4 + Cl_2 \longrightarrow CH_3Cl + HCl$
- **Reaction type:** substitution
- **Conditions:** UV light
- **Observations:** chlorine decolourised and misty fumes of HCl produced
- **Mechanism:** free-radical substitution (a series of chain reactions involving several steps)

Mechanism for the chlorination of methane

Initiation

This is the homolytic bond fission of the bond in the chlorine molecule to produce chlorine free radicals:

$Cl_2 \longrightarrow 2Cl\bullet$

Propagation

A molecule and a radical react to produce another molecule and a radical. The continued formation of radicals propagates the reaction. No H• radicals are produced:

$CH_4 + Cl\bullet \longrightarrow CH_3\bullet + HCl$

$CH_3\bullet + Cl_2 \longrightarrow CH_3Cl + Cl\bullet$

$CH_3Cl + Cl\bullet \longrightarrow CH_2Cl\bullet + HCl$

$CH_2Cl\bullet + Cl_2 \longrightarrow CH_2Cl_2 + Cl\bullet$

This process continues until CCl_4 is produced.

Overall equation: $CH_4 + 4Cl_2 \longrightarrow CCl_4 + 4HCl$

Termination

As the concentration of free radicals increases, there is a greater chance of two colliding to produce a stable molecule:

$CH_3\bullet + CH_3\bullet \longrightarrow C_2H_6$
$CH_3\bullet + Cl\bullet \longrightarrow CH_3Cl$

Final products

- A mixture of haloalkanes (CH_3Cl, CH_2Cl_2, $CHCl_3$, CCl_4) is produced by the chlorination of methane.
- If excess methane is used then CH_3Cl is the major product.

With other alkanes:

- when ethane is chlorinated, the mono-chloro derivative is chloroethane
- when propane is chlorinated, there are two possible mono-chloro derivatives — 1-chloropropane and 2-chloropropane
- butane reacts with bromine in the presence of UV light to produce 1-bromobutane and 2-bromobutane as mono-bromo products

Similar reactions take place with other alkanes and other halogens.

Alkenes and epoxyethane

You should be able to describe the structure and bonding in alkenes, i.e. know that they all contain a double C=C bond which is a region of high electron density.

The chemistry of alkenes is dominated by the C=C bond and its ability to undergo **addition reactions**. You need to be able to write equations and give mechanisms for the electrophilic addition reactions with HBr, H_2SO_4 and Br_2.

You should be able to predict the major and minor products when unsymmetrical alkenes undergo addition reactions and explain the formation of the final product by referring to the relative stabilities of the carbocation intermediates.

The industrial importance of alkenes is illustrated by their addition reactions with hydrogen and water. You should be able to predict the products of the addition polymerisation of alkenes.

The final section is the most difficult. It deals with the production of epoxyethane from ethene and the hydrolysis of epoxyethane with water and alcohols.

Structure and bonding in alkenes

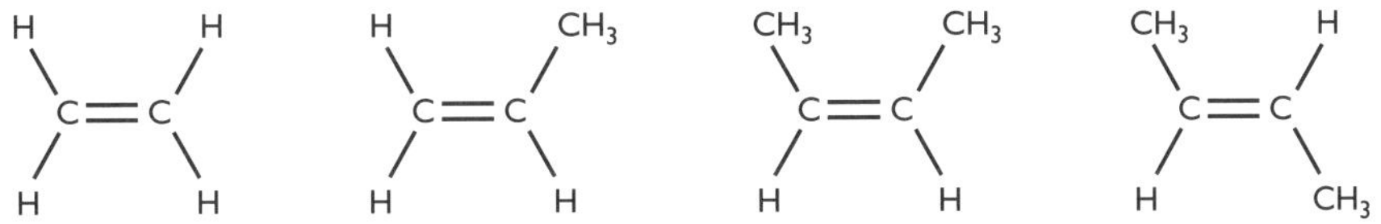

Ethene Propene *cis*-But-2-ene *trans*-But-2-ene

- The alkenes shown above all belong to the same homologous series. They have the same general formula $\mathbf{C_nH_{2n}}$. They have very similar chemical properties and show a gradual change in their physical properties.
- All the alkenes are **unsaturated**, i.e. they contain a carbon–carbon double bond.
- The three atoms attached to a carbon atom involved in a C=C bond are arranged in a **trigonal planar** fashion.
- The **non-rotational** C=C bond leads to **geometrical isomerism** in some alkenes.
- The presence of the C=C bond can be confirmed by adding **bromine water**, which is rapidly **decolourised**.

The reactive nature of alkenes

- The C=C bond contains a strong sigma (σ) bond and a weaker pi (π) bond.
- It is the weaker π bond in alkenes which breaks to allow alkenes to be more reactive than alkanes and undergo **addition** reactions.
- Alkenes contain a region of **high electron density** between the carbon atoms involved in the C=C bond.
- Alkenes are readily attacked by **electrophiles** (**electron pair acceptors** which are seeking out an electron-rich site).
- The chemistry of alkenes is dominated by **electrophilic addition**.

Electrophilic addition to symmetrical alkenes

You need to be able to write equations and mechanisms for electrophilic additions involving any alkene. In the first two examples below, but-2-ene has been used. In the third example, ethene has been used because questions on addition followed by the hydrolysis of the product are quite common. It is essential that in each case you can draw the three curly arrows in their correct positions, so that you can gain the 3 marks awarded for a correct mechanism.

Example 1: reaction with HBr

- **Conditions:** alkene and gaseous HBr or concentrated aqueous HBr
- **Typical equation:** $CH_3CH{=}CHCH_3 + HBr \longrightarrow CH_3CH_2CHBrCH_3$
- **Mechanism:**

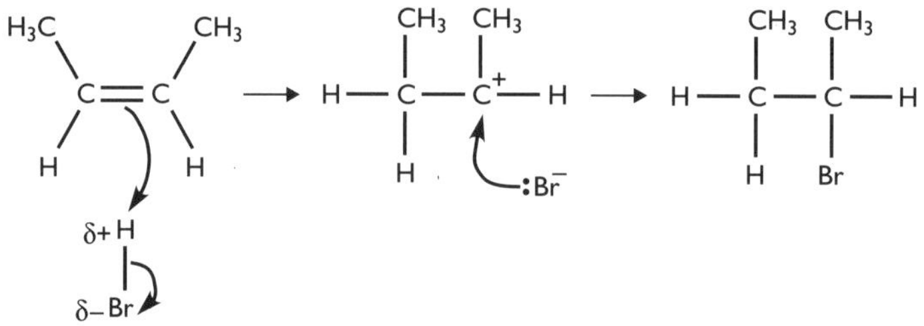

The HBr molecule has a permanent dipole because of the differing electronegativities of hydrogen and bromine. The HBr will readily accept an electron pair from the region of high electron density in the alkene.

Example 2: reaction with bromine

- **Conditions:** alkene and Br_2 in an organic solvent
- **Typical equation:** $CH_3CH{=}CHCH_3 + Br_2 \longrightarrow CH_3CHBrCHBrCH_3$
- **Mechanism:**

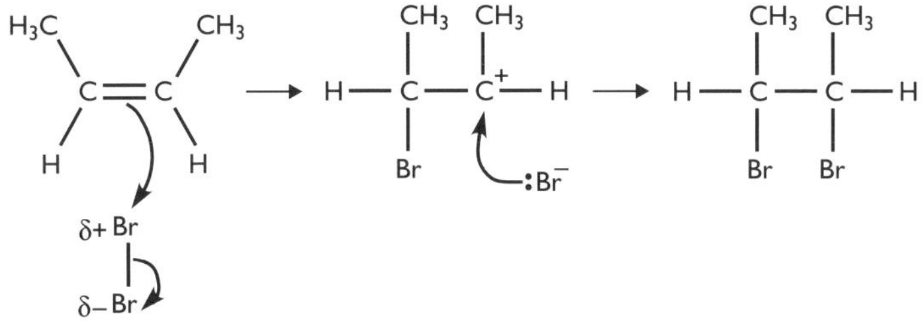

The Br–Br bond is usually non-polar and breaks homolytically, but in this reaction, when it approaches the double bond, it has an induced dipole (i.e. the electron distribution in the bromine molecule becomes unequal because it is affected by the region of high electron density in the alkene). The Br–Br bond breaks **heterolytically** and a bromide ion is produced, which attacks the positive intermediate. When bromine water is used, another possible product is formed because H_2O acts as a nucleophile and attacks the positively charged intermediate to produce $CH_3CHBrCH(OH)CH_3$.

Example 3: reaction with sulphuric acid

- **Conditions:** alkene and cold, concentrated sulphuric acid produces the alkyl hydrogensulphate; if this is warmed in dilute sulphuric acid, the alcohol is produced
- **Typical equations:** $CH_2{=}CH_2 + H_2SO_4 \longrightarrow CH_3CH_2OSO_3H$
  $CH_3CH_2OSO_3H + H_2O \longrightarrow CH_3CH_2OH + H_2SO_4$
- **Mechanism:**

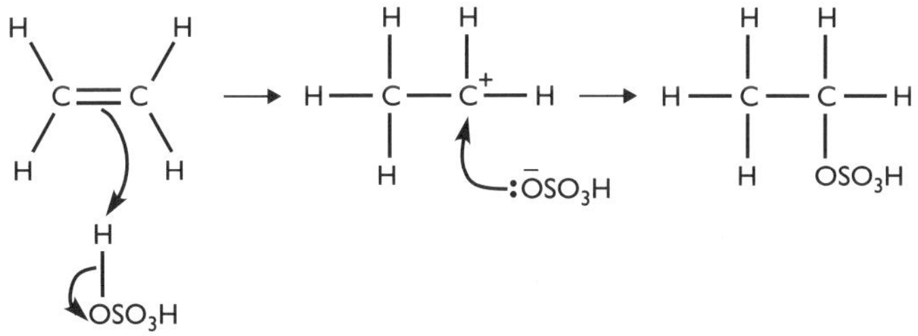

The addition of sulphuric acid to ethene results in the formation of ethyl hydrogensulphate. This then undergoes hydrolysis to produce ethanol. The two reactions represent the overall addition of water to an alkene to form an alcohol.

Electrophilic addition to unsymmetrical alkenes

- When an unsymmetrical reagent of the type HX (e.g. H–Br, H–Cl, H–OSO_3H) reacts with an unsymmetrical alkene, there are two possible products. The **major product** is formed via the **most stable carbocation** (carbonium ion).
- The order of stability of carbocations is tertiary (3°) > secondary (2°) > primary (1°).

- Some examples of carbocations are shown below:

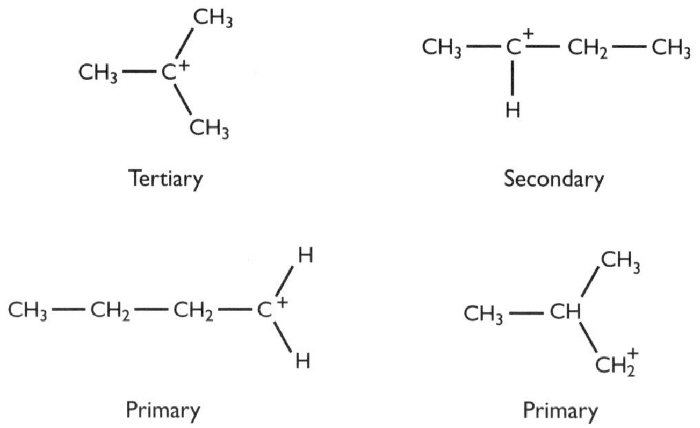

Example 1: addition of hydrogen bromide (HBr) to propene

The two possible products are 1-bromopropane and 2-bromopropane. The **major product** is 2-bromopropane, because it forms via the **more stable secondary carbocation**. The **minor product** is 1-bromopropane, because it forms via the **less stable primary carbocation**.

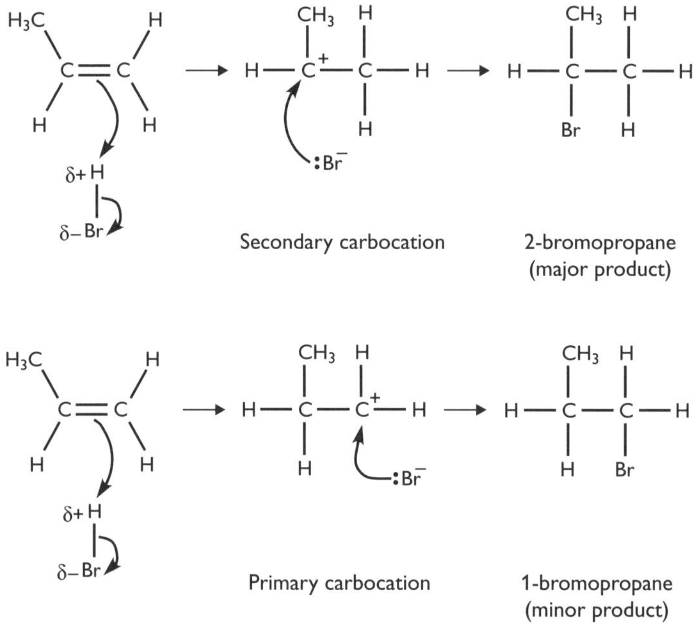

Example 2: addition of sulphuric acid (H_2SO_4) to methylpropene

There are two possible products. However, the only product formed is via the **tertiary carbocation**, which is far more stable than the other possible product formed via the primary carbocation. **Hydrolysis** of the major product, with dilute sulphuric acid, produces **2-methylpropan-2-ol**.

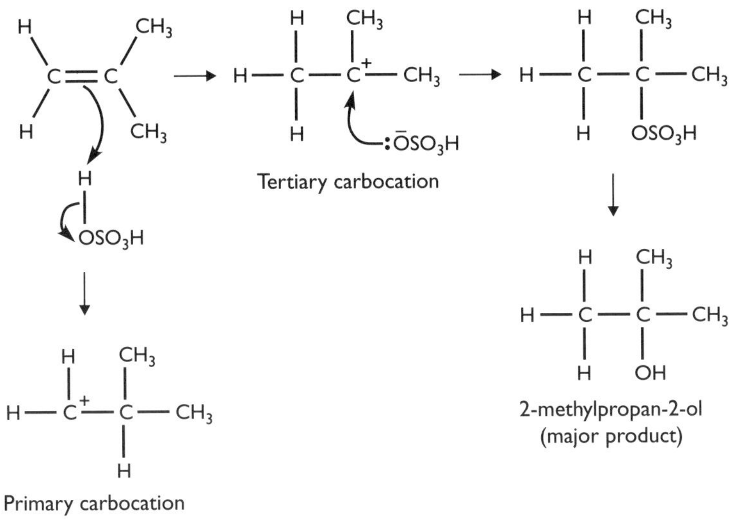

Industrial importance of alkenes

There are three industrial processes involving ethene that you need to consider:

- **hydration** — the addition of water, in the presence of an acid catalyst
- **hydrogenation** — the addition of hydrogen in the presence of a nickel catalyst
- **polymerisation** — the linking together of many ethene molecules to form poly(ethene)

Hydration of ethene

- **Conditions:** steam, 300 °C, 6.5 MPa
- **Product:** ethanol
- **Equation:**

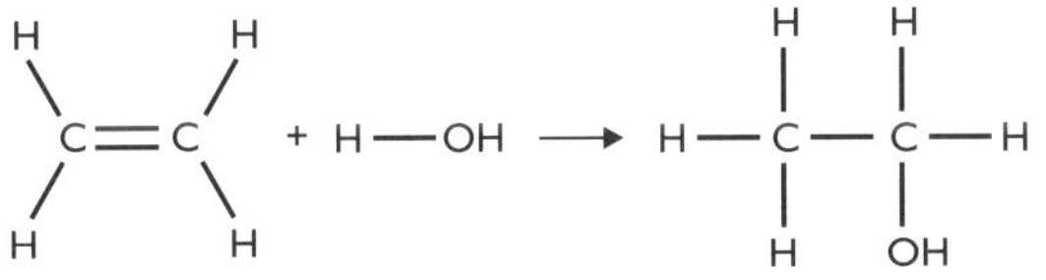

Hydrogenation of ethene

- **Conditions:** finely divided nickel catalyst, 150 °C
- **Product:** ethane
- **Equation:**

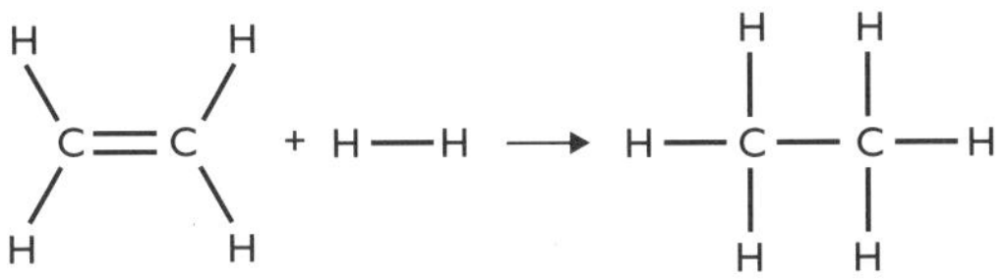

This type of reaction is used to harden vegetable oils to form solid fats in margarine manufacture. The oils contain unsaturated compounds which are converted to saturated compounds. The hardness of the margarine depends upon the amount of hydrogen used.

Polymerisation of ethene

- **Conditions:** ethene is put under pressure in the presence of an oxygen catalyst. Other possible catalysts include $TiCl_4$ and $Al(C_2H_5)_3$.
- **Product:** polyethene (a long-chain, **saturated** molecule)
- **Equation:**

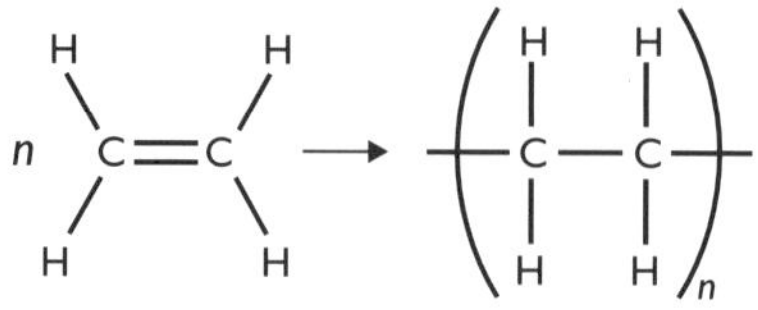

The above reaction is an example of **addition polymerisation**.

All alkenes have the ability to undergo addition polymerisation because of the presence of the double bond. The alkene is the **monomer**. When a large number of monomers join together they form a long-chain **polymer**. The polymer is called a **polyalkene**, but it is a saturated molecule.

You need to be able to predict the structures of other addition polymers from the structure of the monomer. For example, the polymerisation of propene is shown below.

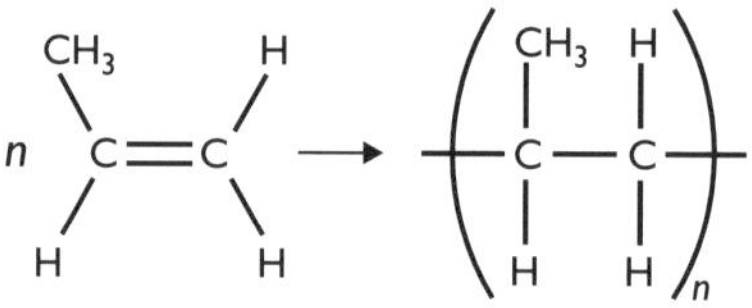

The production and reactions of epoxyethane

This is one of the most difficult sections in Module 3. The information is broken down into a series of small sections so that it is much easier to revise.

Preparation

Epoxyethane is a very reactive compound, commonly known as **ethylene oxide**. It is produced on a large scale by the **partial oxidation of ethene**. Ethene is reacted with **oxygen** or air in the presence of a **silver-based catalyst**. 20% of the ethene is lost as CO_2 and H_2O.

- **Conditions:** 250–300 °C, 1–2 MPa, silver-based catalyst
- **Equation:**

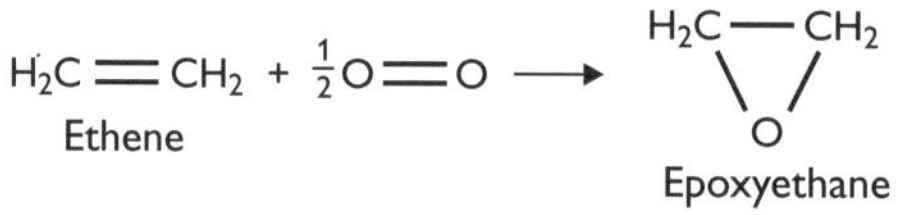

Hazards associated with epoxyethane

- It is a colourless gas, which is **flammable** and **explosive**.
- It is **toxic** and may cause respiratory system irritation as well as neurological effects.

Uses of epoxyethane

- It is an excellent **sterilising** agent.
- Its main use is in the **synthesis of ethane-1,2-diol** and in the preparation of surfactants (detergents).

High reactivity of epoxyethane

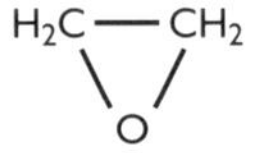

- The **strained** 3-membered ring in epoxyethane makes it highly reactive towards nucleophiles (electron pair donors), such as water and alcohols.
- These **hydrolysis** reactions are very **exothermic** and the bond breaks to open the ring.

Reaction of epoxyethane with water

- Epoxyethane is treated with excess water at 60 °C in the presence of concentrated sulphuric acid.
- It reacts with water to produce **ethane-1,2-diol (ethylene glycol)**.

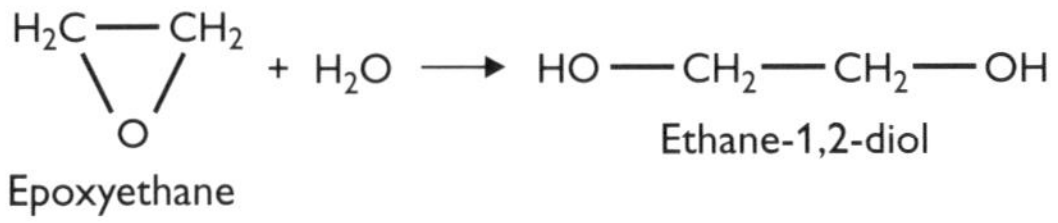

Ethane-1,2-diol is used:

- in the manufacture of the polymer, **terylene**
- as an **antifreeze** in cars; it has ideal properties of low freezing point, high boiling point and being miscible with water

Formation of polyethylene glycols

If the proportion of water is lowered in the reaction between water and epoxyethane, more complex polymeric products are produced. This is because the initial products attack the epoxyethane again.

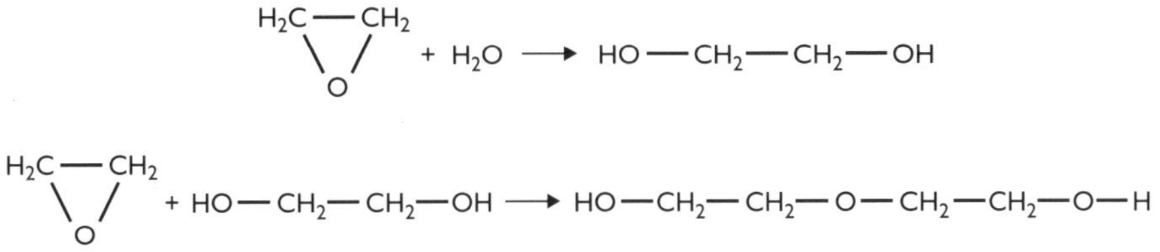

The overall reaction is shown below:

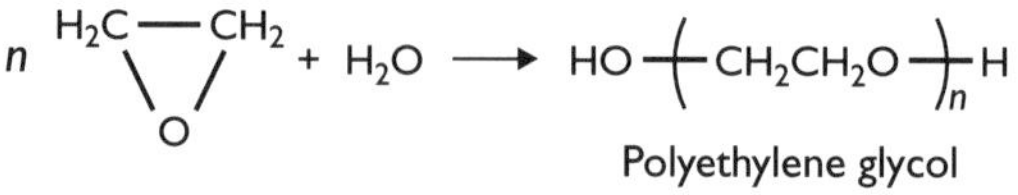

Polyethylene glycol

Polyethylene glycols are used in the manufacture of **plasticisers**, polyester **resins**, **solvents** and **lubricants**.

Reactions of epoxyethane with alcohols

- These are similar to the reaction of epoxyethane with water.
- The most common alcohols used are methanol, ethanol and butan-1-ol.
- They react to form **monoalkylethers**.

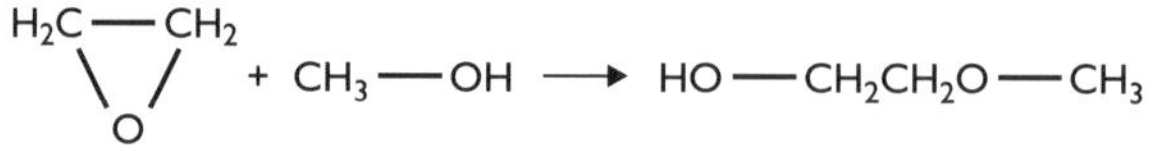

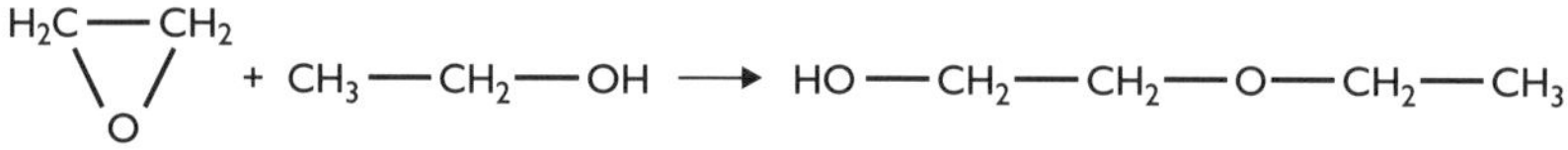

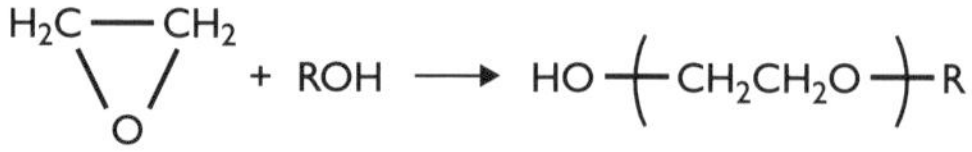

Production and uses of polyalkylethers

Even with a large excess of alcohol, polymerisation still occurs in a similar fashion to the reaction with water. The reaction is summarised by the following equation:

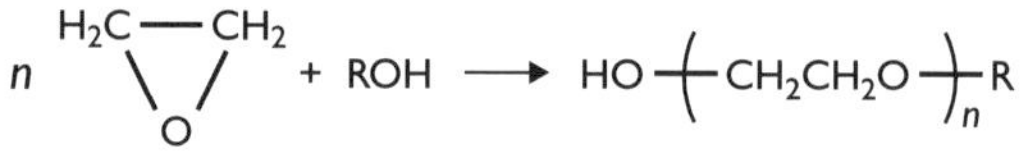

Polyalkylethers are used as **solvents** in paints and in printing inks. The more complex products are used as **plasticisers** and in brake fluids.

Non-ionic **detergents** are produced by the reaction of long-chain alcohols with a large excess of epoxyethane. A typical structure is shown below:

$$HO—(CH_2CH_2O)_9—CH_2—(CH_2)_{10}—CH_3$$

Reaction with other nucleophiles

Epoxyethane reacts with other nucleophiles, such as ammonia.

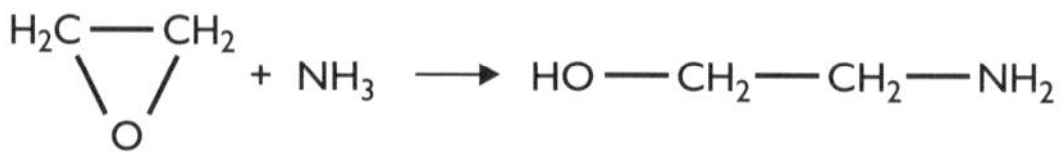

Epoxyethane

Haloalkanes

You need to understand that the polar nature of haloalkanes makes them susceptible to attack by nucleophiles such as OH^-, CN^- and NH_3. You need to be able to explain how these three nucleophiles attack the haloalkane. For each reaction, you should be able to describe the mechanism, give the conditions and write the equation.

The importance of haloalkanes in synthetic routes is tested by questions that ask you to use CN^- to produce a nitrile from a haloalkane and to describe how the nitrile produced is hydrolysed to produce a carboxylic acid.

The final section on haloalkanes is the most difficult. You need to be able to describe the role of the OH^- ion in the reactions of haloalkanes that produce alkenes (via elimination) and alcohols (via substitution).

Nomenclature

Haloalkanes are organic compounds containing a halogen atom such as fluorine, chlorine, bromine or iodine.

Haloalkanes are classified as **primary**, **secondary** or **tertiary**. This depends upon the number of alkyl groups attached to the carbon bearing the halogen. A primary haloalkane has one alkyl group attached, a secondary haloalkane has two alkyl groups and a tertiary haloalkane has three alkyl groups.

Primary (1°)

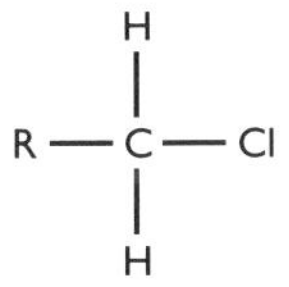

Secondary (2°)

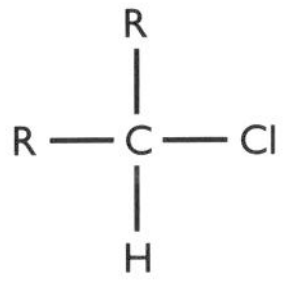

Tertiary (3°)

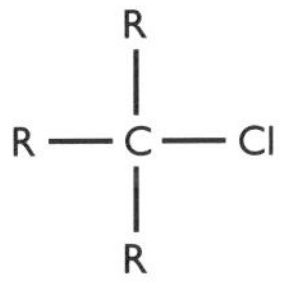

R represents any length of hydrocarbon chain (e.g. CH_3, C_2H_5, C_3H_7)

It is important that you can name and classify each of the haloalkanes shown below.

Bromoethane (1°)

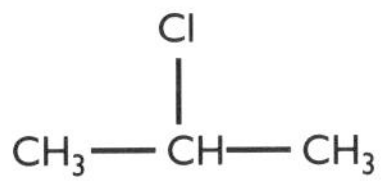

2-chloropropane (2°)

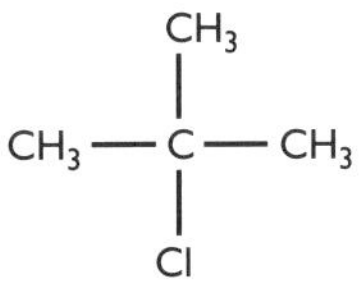

2-chloro-2-methylpropane (3°)

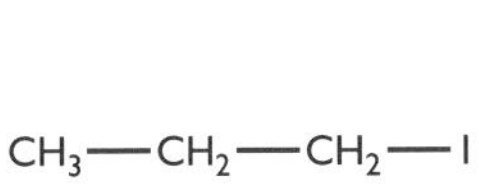

1-iodopropane (1°)

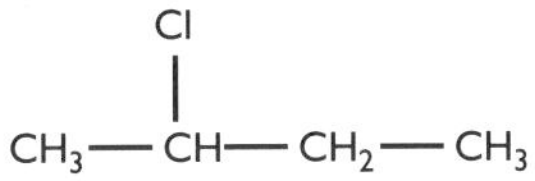

2-chlorobutane (2°)

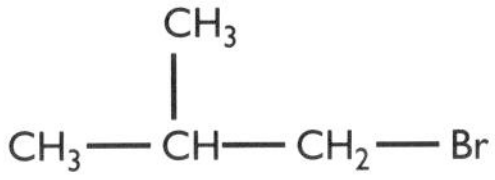

1-bromo-2-methylpropane (1°)

Nucleophilic substitution

Reactive site

- The carbon–halogen bond in a haloalkane is **polar** because of the difference in electronegativity between the carbon and halogen atoms.
- The high electronegativity of the halogen atom causes the carbon to become **electron-deficient** (shown by δ+) and the halogen atom to become electron-rich (shown by δ–). The electron-deficient carbon atom is attacked readily by **nucleophiles** (electron pair donors).
- The nucleophile forms a bond with the carbon and the halogen leaves as a stable halide ion.

Mechanism

- **Nucleophilic substitution** is the replacement of a halogen atom by a nucleophile (electron pair donor) in which the nucleophile attacks the electron-deficient carbon atom.
- In the general mechanism shown below, the nucleophile is represented by the symbol $:Nu^-$. This mechanism could be used for the reaction between a haloalkane and $:OH^-$ or $:CN^-$ ions. The reaction with ammonia is more complicated and is shown later.

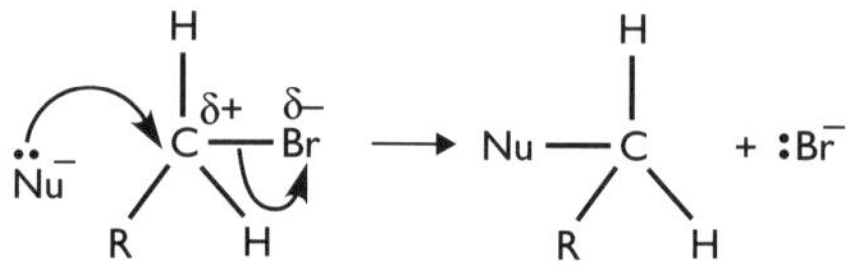

The examiner will be checking to see that the lone pair of electrons is in the correct position on the nucleophile. It is essential that the curly arrow from the nucleophile starts at the lone pair and finishes somewhere near the electron-deficient carbon atom. The curly arrow starting at the bond and finishing at the bromine atom shows the breaking of the C–Br bond. The polarity of the C–Br bond is also shown.

You only need to know the mechanism for nucleophilic substitution in primary haloalkanes.

Rate of nucleophilic substitution

There are two possible factors that could influence the rate of substitution in haloalkanes:

- **Polarity** — the more polar the bond, the more electron-deficient the carbon atom, so the more susceptible it is to attack by nucleophiles. The C–F bond is the most polar and the C–I bond is the least polar.
- **Bond strength** — the longer the carbon–halogen bond, the weaker it is, so the greater the chance of the bond breaking and the halide ion leaving. The C–F bond is the shortest and strongest; the C–I bond is the longest and weakest.

The rate of substitution found by experiment is:

iodoalkanes > bromoalkanes > chloroalkanes > fluoroalkanes

This means that the **bond strength** is the most important factor in determining the rate of nucleophilic substitution in haloalkanes.

Examples of nucleophilic substitution

You need to be able to recall the reagents, conditions, equations and mechanisms for three examples of nucleophilic substitution.

Example 1: hydrolysis of haloalkanes to alcohols

- **Reagents:** aqueous sodium or potassium hydroxide, NaOH(aq) or KOH(aq)
- **Conditions:** reflux in aqueous solvent
- **Example:** 1-bromopropane reacts with NaOH to produce propan-1-ol
- **Equation:** $CH_3CH_2CH_2Br + NaOH \longrightarrow CH_3CH_2CH_2OH + NaBr$
- **Mechanism:**

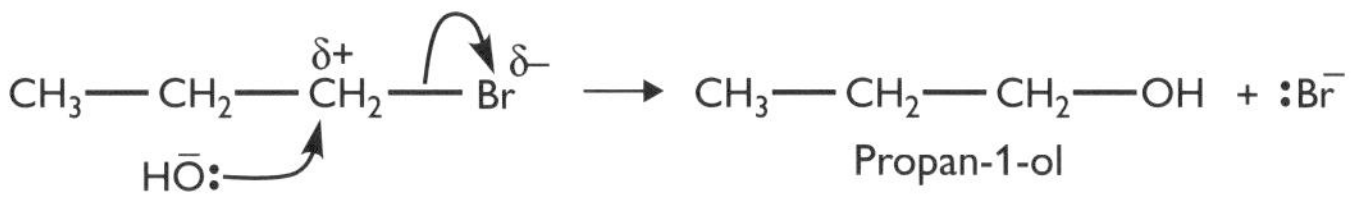

Example 2: conversion of haloalkanes into nitriles

- **Reagents:** sodium or potassium cyanide, NaCN or KCN
- **Conditions:** reflux in an aqueous/alcoholic solvent
- **Example:** 1-bromopropane reacts with NaCN to produce butanenitrile
- **Equation:** $CH_3CH_2CH_2Br + NaCN \longrightarrow CH_3CH_2CH_2CN + NaBr$
- **Mechanism:**

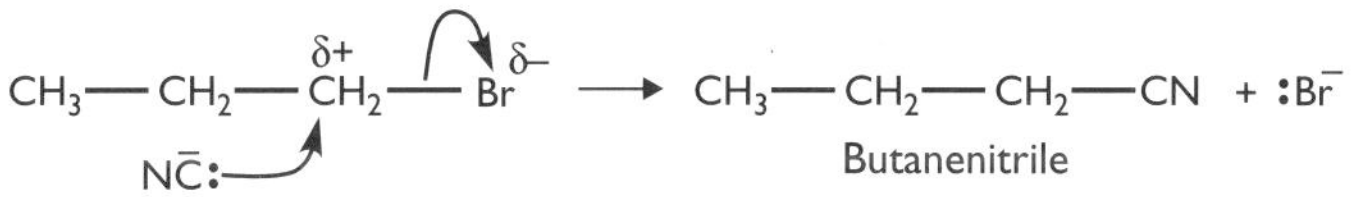

The nitrile produced can be converted to a carboxylic acid by hydrolysis. It is refluxed with dilute hydrochloric acid.

$$CH_3CH_2CH_2CN + 2H_2O + HCl \longrightarrow CH_3CH_2CH_2COOH + NH_4Cl$$

Hydrolysis can also take place in alkaline conditions to produce the salt of the carboxylic acid and ammonia.

$$CH_3CH_2CH_2CN + H_2O + NaOH \longrightarrow CH_3CH_2CH_2COONa + NH_3$$

The nitrile is a useful functional group because it allows the length of the carbon chain to be increased, for example 1-bromo**prop**ane to **but**anoic acid.

Example 3: conversion of haloalkanes into amines

- **Reagents:** ammonia, NH_3
- **Conditions:** ethanol solvent and warmed in a sealed container
- **Example:** 1-bromopropane reacts with NH_3 to produce propylamine

- **Equation:** $CH_3CH_2CH_2Br + 2NH_3 \longrightarrow CH_3CH_2CH_2NH_2 + NH_4Br$
- **Mechanism:**

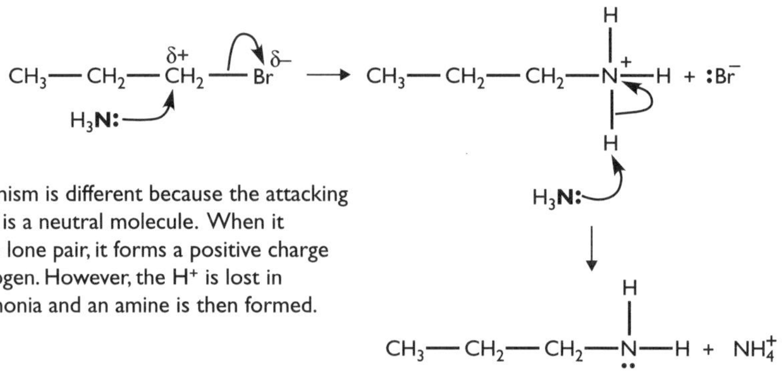

This mechanism is different because the attacking nucleophile is a neutral molecule. When it donates the lone pair, it forms a positive charge on the nitrogen. However, the H^+ is lost in excess ammonia and an amine is then formed.

Substitution and elimination reactions

When a **primary** haloalkane is warmed with NaOH in aqueous conditions, the OH^- ion acts as a nucleophile and donates an electron pair. The OH^- bonds with the carbon to produce an alcohol and the halide ion leaves. Therefore, this reaction is classified as **nucleophilic substitution**.

When a **tertiary** haloalkane reacts with NaOH in a solvent of ethanol at much higher temperatures, the OH^- ion acts as a base and accepts a proton from a carbon atom adjacent to the C–Br bond. The halide ion leaves, leading to the formation of an alkene. This reaction is classified as **elimination**.

A **secondary** haloalkane undergoes **concurrent substitution** and **elimination**. The proportions of alcohol and alkene produced depend upon the solvent (ethanol causes more elimination and water causes more substitution) and the temperature (higher temperatures favour elimination and lower temperatures favour substitution).

Examples of reactions

Example 1: primary haloalkane with sodium hydroxide

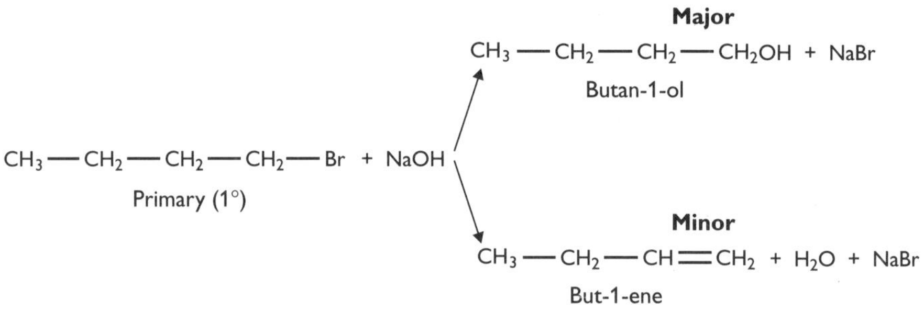

Example 2: tertiary haloalkane with sodium hydroxide

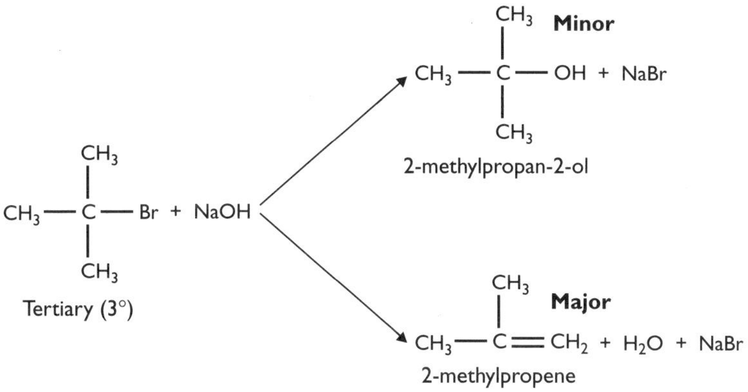

Example 3: secondary haloalkane with sodium hydroxide

A very common question is the reaction of **2-bromobutane**, a secondary haloalkane, with sodium hydroxide under different conditions.

- **Nucleophilic substitution** leads to butan-1-ol. In this reaction, the OH^- acts as a nucleophile by donating an electron pair.
- **Elimination** can lead to but-1-ene, *cis*-but-2-ene and *trans*-but-2-ene. In this reaction, the OH^- acts as a strong base by accepting a proton (H^+ ion) from the haloalkane.

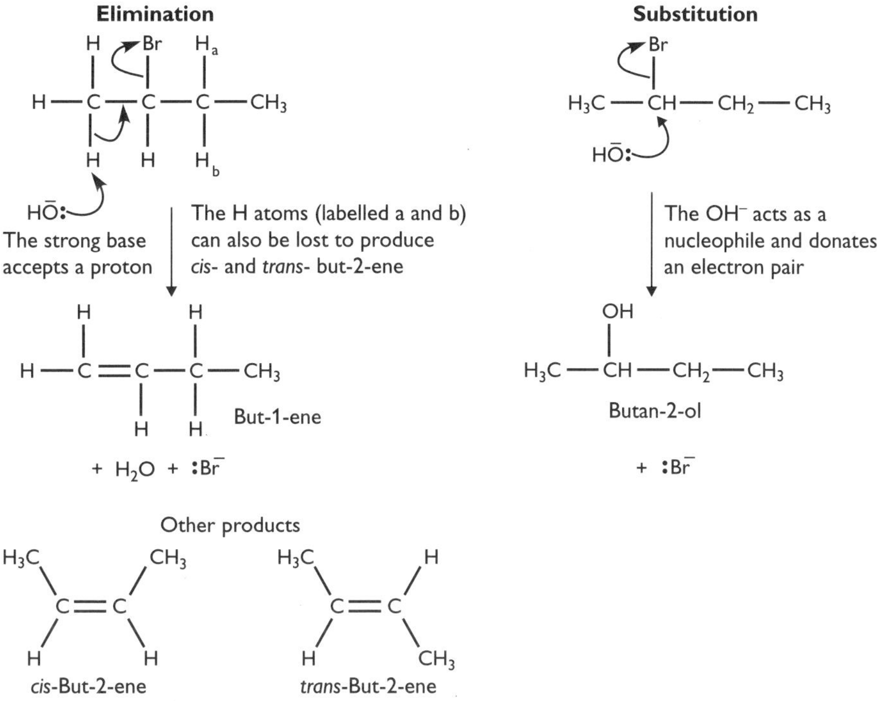

Alcohols

You need to be able to compare the two processes used for the industrial manufacture of ethanol, i.e. fermentation of sugars and hydration of ethene.

You need to be able to name alcohols and classify them as primary, secondary or tertiary. The classification is important because it allows you to predict the products of oxidation. Primary alcohols are oxidised to aldehydes, which can be further oxidised to carboxylic acids. Secondary alcohols are oxidised to ketones and tertiary alcohols are resistant to oxidation.

You need to be able to distinguish between aldehydes and ketones using Fehling's solution or Tollen's reagent. You need to know how to prepare the alcohols by reducing the appropriate carbonyl compound. Aldehydes are reduced to primary alcohols and ketones are reduced to secondary alcohols.

One of the most difficult sections is the elimination of water from alcohols using concentrated sulphuric acid. You need to be able to describe this elimination mechanism in detail.

Industrial manufacture of ethanol

Fermentation

Sugar cane can be converted to ethanol by warming (30–35 °C) in anaerobic conditions in the presence of yeast. An aqueous solution of ethanol (3–15%) is produced which is then purified by fractional distillation.

$$C_6H_{12}O_6 \longrightarrow 2C_2H_5OH + 2CO_2$$

Hydration of ethene

Ethene is hydrated directly using steam and a catalyst of phosphoric acid at 300 °C and 6.5 MPa.

$$CH_2{=}CH_2 + H_2O \longrightarrow CH_3CH_2OH$$

The advantages and disadvantages of the two methods are compared in the table below.

	Fermentation	Hydration
Rate of reaction	Slow	Fast
Quality of product	Impure, low yield	Pure, high yield
Raw material	Sugar is a renewable resource	Ethene is derived from crude oil, which is a finite resource
Process	Batch Expensive on manpower Cheap equipment	Continuous Cheap on manpower Expensive equipment

In the UK, the current method of production of ethanol is via the direct hydration of ethene. However, as crude oil supplies begin to run out, fermentation may become the preferred route.

Nomenclature and classification of alcohols

All alcohols contain the **OH** functional group, which is indicated by the suffix **–ol**. Alcohols are classified as primary (1°), secondary (2°) or tertiary (3°) depending on the number of alkyl groups attached to the carbon atom bearing the OH group.

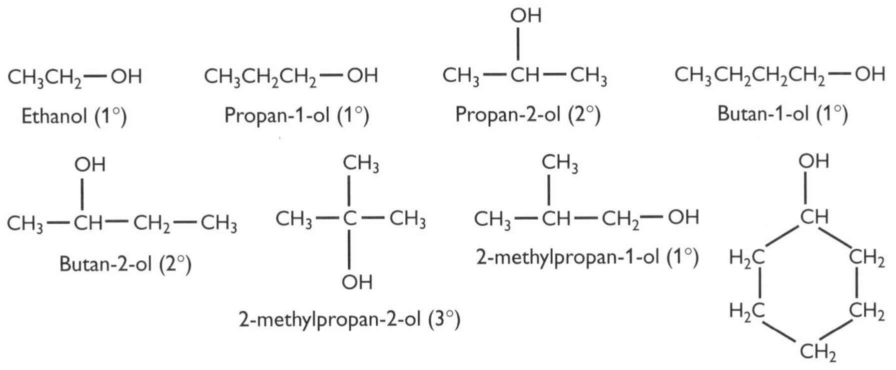

Ethanol (1°); Propan-1-ol (1°); Propan-2-ol (2°); Butan-1-ol (1°); Butan-2-ol (2°); 2-methylpropan-2-ol (3°); 2-methylpropan-1-ol (1°); Cyclohexanol (2°)

Reactions of alcohols

Oxidation of alcohols to carbonyl compounds

- Primary and secondary alcohols are oxidised by suitable oxidising agents such as acidified potassium dichromate(VI), $K_2Cr_2O_7$ or acidified potassium manganate(VII), $KMnO_4$. The acid used is usually dilute sulphuric.
- The oxidising agents are reduced and undergo a colour change. Potassium dichromate is reduced from $Cr_2O_7^{2-}$ to $2Cr^{3+}$, causing the colour to change from orange to green. Potassium manganate(VII) is reduced from MnO_4^- to Mn^{2+} and the colour changes from purple to colourless.
- The equations in this section are simplified by the use of **[O]** to represent the oxidising agent.
- The products of oxidation depend upon the alcohol used and the conditions employed.

Oxidation of primary alcohols

Distillation — the **aldehyde** forms and is distilled off to prevent further oxidation.

Example: the conversion of **ethanol** to **ethanal**

$CH_3CH_2OH + [O] \longrightarrow CH_3CHO + H_2O$

Reflux — the initial aldehyde product is further oxidised to produce a **carboxylic acid**.
Example: the conversion of **ethanol** to **ethanoic acid**

$CH_3CH_2OH + 2[O] \longrightarrow CH_3COOH + H_2O$

Oxidation of secondary alcohols

The alcohol is refluxed to produce a **ketone**.
Example: the conversion of **propan-2-ol** to **propanone**

$CH_3CH(OH)CH_3 + [O] \longrightarrow CH_3COCH_3 + H_2O$

Oxidation of tertiary alcohols

Tertiary alcohols are **resistant to oxidation** under these conditions. When warmed with acidified potassium dichromate, the solution does *not* undergo a colour change, i.e. it remains orange.

Distinguishing between the products of oxidation

The following distinguishing tests depend upon the fact that **aldehydes are stronger reducing agents** than ketones. Aldehydes are easily oxidised to carboxylic acids, but ketones are resistant to oxidation by mild oxidising agents. The aldehyde still possesses a hydrogen atom that can be oxidised to an OH group, thus producing a carboxylic acid.

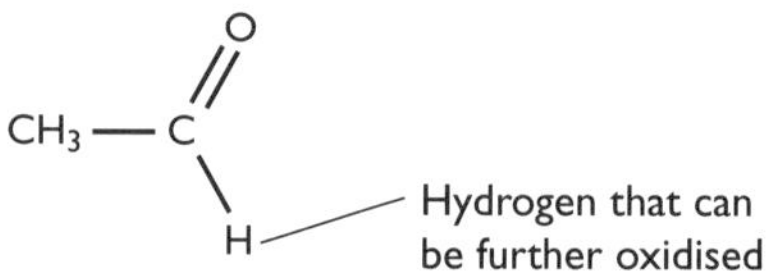

Aldehyde

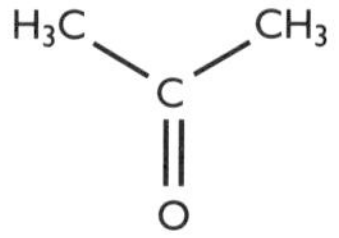

Ketone

Use of Tollen's reagent (the silver mirror test)

- **Reagents:** silver nitrate and ammonia solution
- **Procedure:** Ammonia solution is added to silver nitrate until the brown precipitate of silver oxide dissolves, producing a colourless solution, which contains the complex ion $[Ag(NH_3)_2]^+$. This solution is added to the aldehyde and if there is no reaction, the mixture is gently warmed.
- **Equation:** $CH_3CHO + [O] \longrightarrow CH_3COOH$
- **Observations:** The silver complex is reduced to produce a **metallic silver precipitate**. A ketone gives no reaction.

Use of Fehling's solution

- **Reagents:** Fehling's A and B solution, which is a mixture of copper(II) sulphate solution and sodium potassium tartrate in excess sodium hydroxide. The reagents combine to produce a deep blue solution containing a complex Cu^{2+} ion.
- **Procedure:** The solution is added to the aldehyde and warmed gently.
- **Equation:** $CH_3CHO + [O] \longrightarrow CH_3COOH$

- **Observations:** The Cu^{2+} complex is reduced to a **red precipitate** of **copper(I) oxide, Cu_2O**. A ketone gives no reaction.

Reduction of carbonyl compounds to alcohols

The products of the oxidation of alcohols are readily converted back again to the alcohols by reduction with **sodium tetrahydridoborate(III), $NaBH_4$** in methanol.

To simplify the equations, **[H]** is used to represent the reducing agent.

Reduction of aldehydes

- Aldehydes are reduced to primary alcohols.
- Propanal gives propan-1-ol.
- $CH_3CH_2CHO + 2[H] \longrightarrow CH_3CH_2CH_2OH$

Reduction of ketones

- Ketones are reduced to secondary alcohols.
- Propanone gives propan-2-ol.
- $CH_3COCH_3 + 2[H] \longrightarrow CH_3CH(OH)CH_3$

Reduction of alkenes and carbonyls

- $NaBH_4$ reduces a carbonyl but does not reduce an alkene.
- $CH_2{=}CHCHO + 2[H] \longrightarrow CH_2{=}CHCH_2OH$
- Reduction can also be achieved by using hydrogen with a nickel catalyst. Hydrogen reduces a carbonyl to the alcohol and an alkene to an alkane.
  $CH_2{=}CHCHO + 2H_2 \longrightarrow CH_3CH_2CH_2OH$

Elimination to form alkenes

- **Reagents:** concentrated sulphuric acid (H_2SO_4) or phosphoric acid (H_3PO_4) at 180 °C
- **Examples:** ethanol dehydrates to produce ethene, and propan-2-ol dehydrates to produce propene.
- A common question is predicting the three products of the dehydration of butan-2-ol, i.e. but-1-ene and *cis*- and *trans*-but-2-ene.

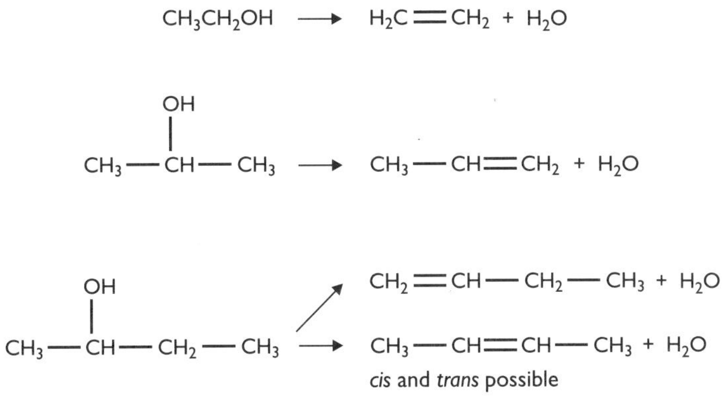

- **Mechanism:** this involves the loss of a proton from a carbocation generated from a protonated alcohol. The example below shows the dehydration of propan-2-ol.

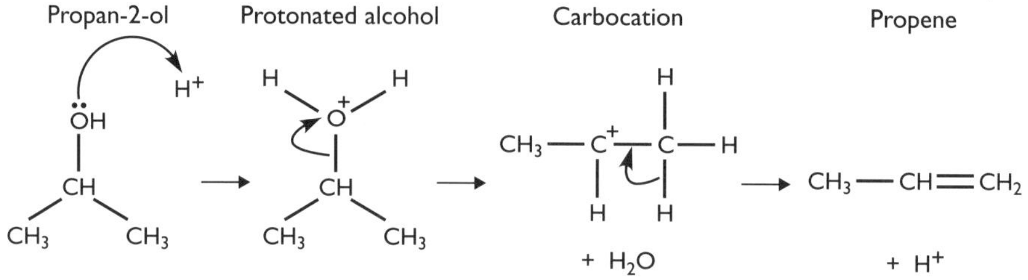

The OH group on the alcohol accepts an H^+ ion from the acid and becomes protonated. This creates H_2O^+, which readily takes an electron pair and leaves as H_2O. The resulting carbocation then loses an H^+ ion from the carbon atom adjacent to that which lost the H_2O. When the H^+ leaves, the electron pair moves, forming a double bond.

Practical work

This half-unit represents 15% of the total AS marks or 7.5% of the total A-level marks. It can be assessed in two different ways; your teacher will have chosen the best route for you and your fellow students.

Centre-assessed coursework

Centre-assessed coursework requires your teacher to assess your performance in four skill areas: planning (P), implementing (I), analysing (A) and evaluating (E). Coursework is completed during normal timetabled lessons. It should be carried out under exam conditions with all the work being done in the practical sessions. You have to produce at least 2 mark scores for each skill area, from different units. Your teacher will select the best marks. The marks for all four skill areas cannot be selected from the same unit. There are 8 marks available for each of skills P, I and A; 6 marks for skill E. Consider the example below.

Practical	Unit	P	I	A	E
Determining the amount of aminosulphonic acid in coffee descaler by titration	1	<u>7</u>	5	6	4
Estimating the strength of a weak acid by its enthalpy of neutralisation	2	6	<u>7</u>	<u>8</u>	<u>5</u>

In this example, the score is 27 marks out of a possible 30. At least 1 mark score has come from a different unit, so the criteria specified by the AQA exam board have been fulfilled. There is no limit to the amount of practical work that can be done; many students want to be assessed several times in order to aim for the full 30 marks. In my experience, this is a waste of time. You are advised to spend more time preparing for the Unit 3(a) test, which is 25% of the total AS marks. A coursework mark of over 26 out of 30 marks is the quality of work expected from a grade-A candidate — so relax!

Many centres opt for the centre-assessed coursework because students are more relaxed and also they have several opportunities to produce their best mark. The main disadvantage of the centre-assessed coursework is that it is very time-consuming.

The practical examination

The practical exam lasts for 2 hours and assesses the same four skills of planning (P), implementing (I), analysing (A) and evaluating (E). These skills are assessed once during the exam using the same criteria as the centre-assessed coursework. The exercises in the practical exam are not as demanding as those used in the centre-assessed coursework. However, before you think the practical exam is a soft option, remember that the exam is completed in a limited amount of time and all the exercises you meet will be totally unfamiliar.

Marking the assessments

All the practical assessments (and the practical exam) should have been written in a way that makes it clear what you need to do to achieve full marks. However, in order to prepare for the assessments, it is useful to have an understanding of the criteria used to mark each skill area and of how many marks are allocated to each section. The marks allocated will vary from practical to practical. However, those shown below should give you a rough guide as to the importance of each section within each skill area.

Planning

Scale (2 marks)

This involves a calculation to predict how much substance is used in the practical. This is the most difficult section in planning, so if you cannot attempt this section then ask for help.

Method (3 marks)

If the assessment involves a titration, then you should describe how to prepare a standard solution and how to carry out a titration.

Use of results (2 marks)

You need to demonstrate how to use your results to calculate the final answer.

Safety (1 mark)

You need to consider the hazards and precautions associated with the practical you plan to carry out. These should not be general safety precautions; they should be specific to this practical.

Implementing

Manipulative skills (2 or 3 marks)

Your technique is assessed during the practical session. You are assessed on your ability to weigh out solids accurately, prepare standard solutions, carry out titrations or measure temperature rises.

Recording of results (1 mark)

You need to produce a neat results table by the end of the practical session.

Precision (1 mark)

Results should be expressed to the appropriate number of significant figures. For example, titre readings should be, for example, 25.00 cm^3 and 25.10 cm^3, not 25 cm^3 and 25.1 cm^3.

Accuracy (2 or 3 marks)

The accuracy of your result will be compared with the result obtained by your teacher or the class average. For example, in a simple titration, if your final result is within 1% of the teacher value, you will score full marks.

Analysing

Calculation (4 marks)

If you convert your practical results into the final answer, without any help, then you will score at least 4 marks. This skill area may also involve plotting graphs to estimate the maximum temperature rise in an experiment.

Precision (1 mark)

It is important to quote all your answers to the appropriate number of significant figures. In many titrations or energetics experiments, it is appropriate to quote answers to 3 significant figures. Therefore, if your final answer is 92.3689%, it should be expressed as 92.4% to score the mark for precision.

Errors (2 marks)

You need to be able to estimate the errors in each piece of apparatus used and then add all these errors, to produce a total percentage error for the apparatus used. The accuracy of each piece of apparatus will be given. For example, what is the error in the average titre of 24.50 cm^3 if the accuracy of the burette is $\pm 0.10\ cm^3$?

Answer = $(0.1/24.50) \times 100 = 0.41\%$

Nomenclature and terminology (1 mark)

Take care to present your calculation clearly and logically. Use suitable units in your results table and in your calculation.

Evaluating

Reliability of results (2 marks)

It is quite common to be given a set of results obtained by another student. You have to comment on these results. Is the student's technique satisfactory? Which results were used? Were there any anomalous results?

Drawing conclusions (2 marks)

You should comment on the accuracy of the final answer compared with either a teacher's value or a theoretical value. You have to deduce whether or not the percentage error in the final answer is within the error expected, given the apparatus used in the experiment. You need to identify the major sources of error.

Limitations and improvements (2 marks)

You need to be able to look at the method used in an experiment, identify the main sources of error and suggest ways of improving the experiment to remove these errors.

Examples of practical work

I have not described a full AQA practical assessment because a school or college may use this assessment as part of their coursework. Instead, I have modified different sections from a wide range of assessments to illustrate how each skill is marked.

Planning

Scale

A typical problem involving scale is shown below.

A white powder contains a solid acid (M_r, 97) and some other soluble solid impurities. The acid is monoprotic — i.e. one mole of acid reacts with one mole of an alkali, such as sodium hydroxide. A manufacturer claims that the white powder contains 80% by mass of the solid acid. Plan an experiment to confirm that this is true.

Suggest, with reasons, an appropriate scale for this experiment. You should suggest a sensible concentration for the alkali and use this to calculate the mass of the white powder needed to prepare a standard solution.

A typical marking scheme would involve 8 scoring points and you would need to score all 8 points to achieve full marks on this section. Remember, this section represents 2 marks out of 8 for the planning skill.

- A suitable titre in any titration is $25\,cm^3$. ✓
- A sensible alkali concentration is $0.10\,mol\,dm^{-3}$. ✓
- The number of moles of alkali used in a $25\,cm^3$ portion measured in a pipette and placed in a conical flask will be $0.1 \times 25/1000 = 2.5 \times 10^{-3}$. ✓
- This means the number of moles of acid delivered from the burette to neutralise the alkali will be 2.5×10^{-3} in a $25\,cm^3$ titre. ✓
- The number of moles of acid needed to make a standard solution in a $250\,cm^3$ volumetric flask is 2.5×10^{-2}. ✓
- The M_r of the solid acid is 97, so the mass of white powder weighed out on the electronic balance, assuming the white powder was 100% pure solid acid, is $97 \times 2.5 \times 10^{-2}$ ✓ = 2.43 g. ✓
- So the mass of the white powder needed, assuming the white powder contained 80% of the solid acid by mass, is $2.43 \times 100/80 = 3.04$ g. ✓
- The student should weigh approximately 3.0 g and record the exact mass.

The answers to this section vary, depending on the titre chosen, the concentration of the alkali and the volume of the volumetric flask used to make up the standard solution. However, the principles of the calculation are the same and the marking scheme can be easily adapted to a variety of questions.

Method

Many of the methods in AS practicals involve describing how to prepare a standard solution, followed by using this standard solution in a titration. It is surprising how many students cannot recall the fine detail of the practical procedure necessary to ensure an accurate result in a titration.

Preparing a standard solution

- Wash and clean the apparatus, such as beakers and volumetric flasks, with distilled water.
- Weigh a suitable mass of solid using a weighing boat placed on an electronic balance, which weighs to an accuracy of at least 2 decimal places.
- Dissolve the solid in the minimum amount of distilled water in a 250 cm^3 beaker.
- Rinse the weighing boat with distilled water and add the washings to the beaker.
- Warm and stir the mixture to aid dissolving.
- Transfer the solution to a 250 cm^3 graduated volumetric flask.
- Rinse the beaker and add these washings to the volumetric flask.
- Add more distilled water until the solution reaches the graduation mark on the volumetric flask.
- Stopper the flask and shake it to ensure that the solution has been thoroughly mixed.

Carrying out a titration

- Rinse the equipment with distilled water followed by the reagent to be used, i.e. rinse the pipette with the alkali and the burette with the acid.
- Pipette 25 cm^3 of sodium hydroxide into a conical flask.
- Fill the burette with the acid and remember to remove the funnel from the top of the burette before starting the titration.
- Add a few drops of a named indicator (e.g. phenolphthalein) to the conical flask.
- Note the burette reading at the start of the titration.
- Add the acid from the burette, remembering to swirl the solution in the conical flask.
- Use a white tile to show up the colour change of the indicator.
- Remember to add the acid drop by drop towards the end point.
- Add acid until a permanent colour change is observed.
- Note the burette reading at the end of the titration.
- Repeat the titration until at least two concordant results are obtained.

If you give a perfect answer then you could score up to 3 marks for the method. Remember that the basic method for preparing a standard solution and carrying out a titration is similar in each practical assessment. You will have carried out several titrations when preparing for your assessment, so the detail above will have been covered many times. However, some students still cannot recall the fine detail under exam conditions.

Use of results

Another type of assessment that you might encounter at AS is an enthalpy of neutralisation experiment.

A student planned to mix 25 cm^3 of an acid with 25 cm^3 of sodium hydroxide, both of concentration 2 mol dm^{-3}, in a calorimeter. The temperature was to be monitored to

find the maximum temperature rise. How would this temperature rise be used to determine the enthalpy of neutralisation of the acid?

- Let us assume the temperature rise is 9 °C.
- The heat change is calculated using $q = mc\Delta T$.
- $q = 50 \times 10^{-3} \times 4.18 \times 9 = 1.881$ kJ
- The number of moles of acid used, which is equivalent to the number of moles of water formed, is calculated using $MV/1000$.
- $n = \dfrac{2 \times 25}{1000} = 0.05\,\text{mol}$
- The enthalpy of neutralisation $\Delta H = -q/n$.
- $\Delta H = \dfrac{-1.881}{0.05} = -37.6\,\text{kJ mol}^{-1}$

When strong acids react with sodium hydroxide, the expected enthalpy change is approximately -57 kJ mol^{-1}. Therefore, an answer of -37.6 kJ mol^{-1} allows us to conclude that the acid is a weak acid.

If you show clearly all the points above, you will gain both the available marks for this section of the planning exercise.

Safety

At the end of each planning exercise, you need to consider all the hazards associated with the chemicals used in the experiment and the precautions you would take.

- Acids and alkalis are usually classified as corrosive. However, if they are very dilute, the risks are reduced and they can be classified as irritants.
- Alkalis are particularly dangerous to the eyes, so safety glasses should be warn at all times.
- If acids or alkalis come in contact with the skin, then the affected area must be washed with water immediately.
- Sometimes you are asked to weigh out an unknown compound, which may be acidic or basic. This compound could also be toxic, so the best advice is always to wear plastic gloves to avoid skin contact.

All this advice will have been given to you in practical work throughout the course. However, many students cannot describe in detail the hazards and precautions associated with a particular practical.

Implementing

Manipulative skills

The implementation of the practical is not based on your plan. It is a totally separate exercise. You will be given detailed instructions on how to carry out the practical. Provided that you carry out the practical and show a good range of manipulative skills, and record your results clearly and accurately with a suitable degree of precision, then you will score 5 marks out of a possible 8. Your teacher will use a tick list similar to the one shown below.

In this practical, a student has been asked to make up a standard solution of a solid acid. Then this acid solution has to be mixed with a standard solution of an alkali and the temperature monitored over a 10-minute period. The solutions are mixed at the fourth minute and the student is told not to record the temperature at this point. A typical tick list could be as follows:

Activity	✓
Weighs out solid	
Records the exact mass	
Dissolves in distilled water	
Transfers to volumetric flask	
Makes up to the graduation mark	
Washes equipment appropriately	
Measures out the acid	
Washes and dries the thermometer	
Measures out the alkali	
Cleans and dries the plastic cup	
Cup placed in the polystyrene beaker	
Thermometer always in solution	
Records every minute	
Reads thermometer: teacher checks	
Records results in a clear table	
Records mass used	
Mass between 12.3 g and 12.7 g	
Records temperature of the acid	
Records temperature of the alkali	
No temperature recorded at fourth minute	
Solutions mixed at fourth minute	
Quotes temperature to 0.1 °C	

There are 22 scoring points here. You would need to score over 18 to gain full marks on this section. One skill that students always underestimate is the requirement to present a neat table of results with the individual results expressed to an appropriate degree of accuracy. In the tick list above, the last 8 scoring points are allocated to the presentation of results.

Accuracy of the final result

You could score 5 marks on the skills tick list, so there are 3 marks available for the accuracy of your final experimental result. The accuracy of your result will be compared with either a teacher's value or a class average.

If a student were asked to make up a standard solution and to titrate a portion of this solution against a standard solution of sodium hydroxide, the accuracy of the final result would be marked using the tolerances shown below:

- A result with an error of less than 1.5% when compared with the accepted result scores 3 marks.
- A result with an error between 1.5% and 2.0% scores 2 marks.
- A result with an error between 2.0% and 2.5% scores 1 mark.
- If your work is very inaccurate, then the maximum you can score on the implementing section is 5 out of 8 marks.

Analysing

Calculation

You need to convert your practical results into a final answer, making sure that you show your working out clearly and logically. If you complete the calculation correctly, without any help, then you will score at least 4 of the total 8 marks available for skill A. An example calculation is shown below.

A student was asked to determine the relative formula mass of an unknown acid present in a standard solution of concentration 8.0 g dm^{-3}. The acid solution was placed in the burette and titrated against 25 cm^3 portions of a 0.10 mol dm^{-3} solution of sodium hydroxide.

The following results were obtained.

	Rough	1st	2nd	3rd
Final titre/cm^3	20.50	19.90	39.70	20.40
Initial titre/cm^3	0.00	0.20	19.90	0.50
Titre value/cm^3	20.50	19.70	19.80	19.90

Use the results to calculate the relative formula mass of the unknown acid.

Average titre $= \dfrac{19.7 + 19.8 + 19.9}{3} = 19.80\,\text{cm}^3$

Number of moles of alkali used in the titration $= \dfrac{0.1 \times 25}{1000} = 2.5 \times 10^{-3}$

Number of moles of acid present in the burette $= 2.5 \times 10^{-3}$ in $19.80\,\text{cm}^3$

Number of moles of acid present in $1\,\text{dm}^3 = 2.5 \times 10^{-3} \times \dfrac{1000}{19.80} = 0.126$

Number of moles $n = \dfrac{\text{mass}}{M_r}$

Therefore $M_r = \dfrac{\text{mass}}{n}$

$= \dfrac{8.0}{0.126} = \mathbf{63.5}$

Precision

If you complete the calculation without any help, you will score 4 marks. In order to qualify for the precision mark you must express your answers to the appropriate number of significant figures. Using the example calculation above, there are 3 scoring points that must be covered to achieve the full mark.

- The average titre should be quoted to an accuracy of 0.05 cm^3.
- The molarity of the acid solution should be quoted to 3 significant figures (0.126).
- The M_r should be quoted to 3 significant figures (63.5).

Errors

You have to determine the percentage error in each piece of apparatus used in your experiment. You are expected to total these errors to give a maximum error for the experiment. Finally, you need to calculate the percentage error in your result, compared with the accepted value. The accuracy of each piece of apparatus will be given in the instruction sheet. This section is worth 2 marks.

A student prepared a standard solution of an acid by dissolving 2.53 g of solid in the minimum amount of water. This solution was then transferred, with washings, into a 250 cm^3 volumetric flask. A 25 cm^3 portion of alkali was pipetted into a conical flask and this was titrated against the acid solution, which was added from a burette. The final average titre was 26.50 cm^3.

Assume the maximum errors for the apparatus used in this experiment were:

- **electronic balance ±0.01 g**
- **250 cm^3 volumetric flask ±0.5 cm^3**
- **25 cm^3 pipette ±0.05 cm^3**
- **burette ±0.15 cm^3**

Estimate the maximum percentage error in using each piece of apparatus, and the overall apparatus maximum error.

Error in the electronic balance $= \frac{0.01}{2.53} \times 100 = 0.40\%$

Error in the volumetric flask $= \frac{0.5}{250} \times 100 = 0.20\%$

Error in the pipette $= \frac{0.05}{25} \times 100 = 0.20\%$

Error in the burette $= \frac{0.15}{26.50} \times 100 = 0.57\%$

Total error in the apparatus = 1.37%

You are also expected to calculate the percentage error in your result compared with an accepted value.

A student obtained an enthalpy of neutralisation of –54.3 kJ mol^{-1}. However, the accepted answer was –57.0 kJ mol^{-1}. Calculate the percentage error in the final result.

$$\text{Percentage error} = \frac{\text{accepted answer} - \text{experimental answer}}{\text{accepted answer}} \times 100\%$$

$$\%\ \text{error} = \frac{(57.0 - 54.3)}{57.0} \times 100 = 4.74\%$$

Nomenclature and terminology

This section is worth 1 mark. In order to score this final mark for skill A, you must show a full set of results in a clear table, explain the calculations clearly and logically using a sensible layout, make sure the units are correct and use terminology accurately (e.g. moles must not be confused with molarity or M_r).

Evaluating

This skill is worth 6 marks. It is probably the most difficult section and it is quite common to see poor answers, lacking essential detail. There are three sections, worth 2 marks each.

Reliability of results

You may be provided with a set of sample results, or you could use your own experimental results. You need to comment on the consistency of the results and identify any anomalies.

The student filled a burette with an acid solution. The following results were obtained when 25.00 cm³ portions of 0.10 M sodium hydroxide solution were titrated with the acid solution.

Titration number	1	2	3	4	5
Final burette reading/cm³	26.20	25.30	47.65	25.65	25.35
Initial burette reading/cm³	0.00	0.05	22.30	0.00	0.00

Comment on the consistency of the student's titration results. State which titres were used in calculating the average titre and explain why the other titres were ignored. Suggest one possible reason for an anomalous result.

The student uses titres 2, 3 and 5 and ignores titres 1 and 4, which are outside the accepted tolerance. The student has produced three concordant titres, so the titration technique is good and the results are reliable. Titre 1 is a rough reading and titre 4 is an anomalous result, which could have been caused by adding too much indicator or not swirling the solution in the conical flask during the titration.

Drawing conclusions

You need to be able to comment on the accuracy of your final answer and deduce whether it is within the accepted error for this practical, taking into account the accuracy of the apparatus used. You have to identify the major source of error in the experiment.

In an enthalpy of neutralisation experiment, a student obtained a final result of −38.5 kJ mol^{-1}. However, the accepted value was −50.0 kJ mol^{-1}. The expected accuracy of the experiment from the total error in the apparatus used was 5%.

Calculate the percentage error in the student's result and comment on the magnitude of this error. Suggest the main source of error in this experiment.

$$\% \text{ error} = \frac{(50.0 - 38.5)}{50.0} \times 100 = 23\%$$

This is well outside the maximum percentage error of the apparatus. The main source of error in this experiment is heat loss to the surroundings.

Limitations and improvements

You have to consider the limitations of either your own experimental method or a sample method given to you and then suggest ways of improving the experiment.

For example, in neutralisation experiments the heat loss may be unacceptable and the temperature rise achieved may be too small.

Heat loss can be reduced by adding extra lagging to the sides of the calorimeter and using a lid. Increasing the concentration of the solutions while keeping their volumes the same could increase the temperature rise during the experiment.

The answers to this section vary considerably, depending on the limitations of the experiment. Worksheets should be highly structured and should lead you through the work carefully, so that you are able to identify experimental limitations and suggest improvements.

Questions & Answers

These questions are similar in style and content to those that you can expect in Unit Test 3(a). They have been designed to test the key facts and concepts covered in Module 3(a).

Unit Test 3(a) is divided into sections A and B. Section A questions are structured, with spaces at the end of each question part for your response. Section B usually contains a longer question, which is also divided into sections. It is effectively a long structured question, but with no spaces between each section for you to write your answer.

All the questions in this Question and Answer section are structured, without answer spaces. If a question is worth 12 marks, then you should expect to write no more than 12 sentences. The marking scheme identifies 12 key words or phrases that must be present for you to score the 12 marks.

The questions are worth 30 marks. In Unit Test 3(a), it is rare to find one question concentrating on one topic. However, these 30 marks could represent three separate structured questions, each worth 10 marks, from separate papers. The important point is that if you score well in each test, then at least you can be confident that you understand the topic.

Examiner's comments

Grade-A answers are provided for all questions. These are followed by examiner's comments (preceded by the icon *e*), which point out common errors. They also suggest alternative answers that are acceptable and ways of remembering key points.

In order to use this section effectively, you should:

- make sure you have revised the topic thoroughly before you attempt the question
- read the question carefully and then answer it under test conditions
- use the grade-A answer to assess the quality of your answer — the grade-A answer has been marked by an examiner, with ticks placed where the marks are scored
- read through the examiner's comments to see the common errors made by candidates and tips for improving your answers
- never underestimate the help of your teacher — if you do not understand some of the points made in the answers or the examiner's comments, then ask your teacher (or other students) to explain
- make sure that you concentrate on your weak areas when revising rather than on the topics that you understand

In addition to this guide, use as much material from the AQA exam board as possible. Answer as many past paper questions as you can and then use the mark schemes to grade your answers and analyse your mistakes. As a rough guide, you need to score 80% for a grade A, 70% for a grade B and 60% for a grade C.

Nomenclature and isomerism

(1) (a) Two structural isomers of C_6H_{14} are shown below.

Hexane

$CH_3—CH_2—CH_2—CH_2—CH_2—CH_3$

2-methylpentane

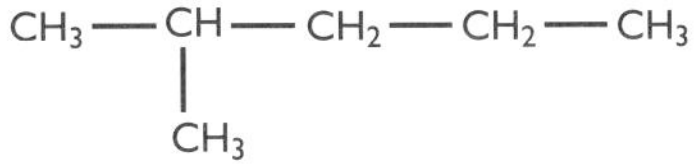

(i) Define the term *empirical formula* and deduce the empirical formula of hexane. (3 marks)

(ii) Define the term *structural isomerism* and state the type of structural isomerism shown by hexane and 2-methylpentane. (3 marks)

(iii) State and explain which compound, hexane or 2-methylpentane, has the lower boiling point. (3 marks)

(iv) Draw and name another *two* structural isomers of C_6H_{14}. (4 marks)

(b) The structures of four isomeric alkenes are shown below.

Compound A

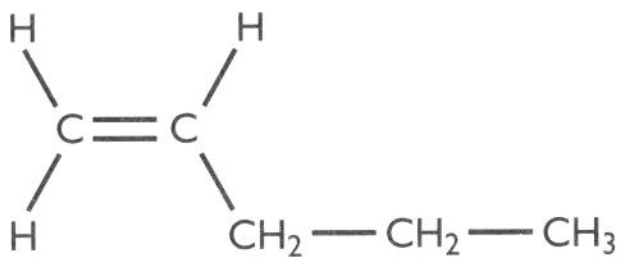

Compound B

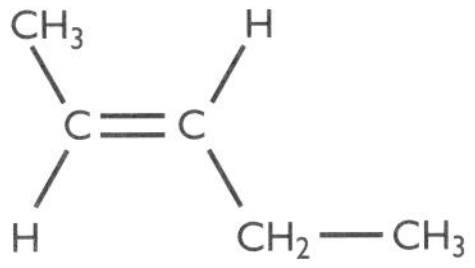

Compound C

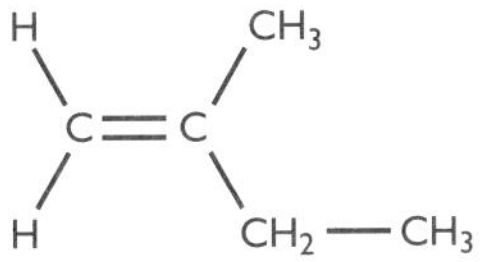

Compound D

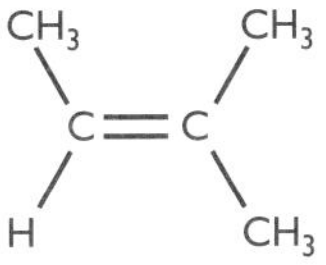

(i) Compounds A to D belong to the same homologous series. Explain the term *homologous series*. (3 marks)

(ii) State the molecular formula of compound A. (1 mark)

(iii) State the empirical formula of compound B. (1 mark)

(iv) Explain the cause of geometrical isomerism that occurs in some alkenes. (2 marks)

(v) Explain why compound C does not show geometrical isomerism. (2 marks)

(vi) Identify *one* of the compounds from A to D that exhibits geometrical isomerism and draw the other geometrical isomer of this compound. (2 marks)

(vii) Draw and name an alkane that is isomeric with compound D. (2 marks)

(c) Draw the structural formula of the following compounds:

(i) pentan-3-one

(ii) propanenitrile

(iii) 3-hydroxybutanal

(iv) cyclohexanol (4 marks)

Total: 30 marks

Grade-A answer to Question 1

(a) (i) The empirical formula is the simplest whole number ratio ✓ of atoms of each element in a compound ✓. The molecular formula is C_6H_{14}, so the empirical formula is C_3H_7 ✓.

The formula C_3H_7 cannot be simplified any further. It must be a whole number ratio.

(ii) Structural isomerism occurs when the molecules have the same molecular formula ✓ but a different structural formula ✓. This type of isomerism is called chain isomerism ✓.

This type of isomerism occurs when there are two or more ways of arranging the carbon skeleton of a molecule.

(iii) 2-methylpentane ✓. The molecule is more branched and so has a lower surface area ✓ and weaker van der Waals forces ✓ between the molecules.

Remember: the more branched the alkane, the lower is its boiling point.

(iv)

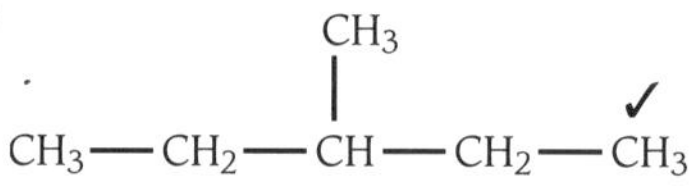

3-methylpentane ✓

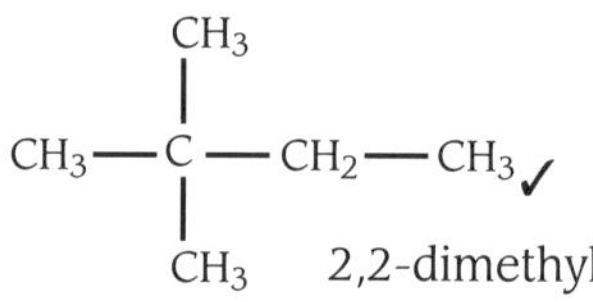

2,2-dimethylbutane ✓

Another possible isomer exists and is an alternative answer:

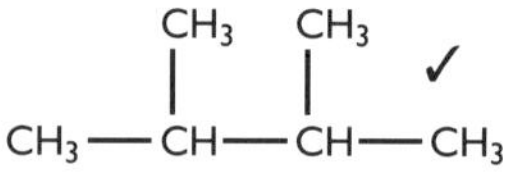

2,3-dimethylbutane ✓

(b) (i) A homologous series is a group of organic compounds with the same general formula ✓ which exhibit very similar chemical properties ✓ because they possess the same functional group ✓. Their physical properties gradually change ✓ (e.g. boiling point increases) as the series is ascended, because the molecules possess an extra CH_2 ✓ group.

There are 5 scoring points here; you need to score 3 to achieve full marks.

(ii) C_5H_{10} ✓

All the alkenes shown here are isomers, so they all have the same molecular formula.

(iii) CH_2 ✓

The ratio of the atoms is 5:10. This simplifies to 1:2, so the empirical formula is CH_2.

(iv) They possess a double bond ✓ which does not rotate ✓.

Always look for the carbon–carbon double bond when predicting the presence of geometrical isomerism.

(v) It has two identical groups ✓ attached to the carbon atom involved in the double bond ✓.

e If a carbon atom involved in the double bond has two hydrogen atoms attached, you will not achieve geometrical isomerism.

(vi) Compound B ✓

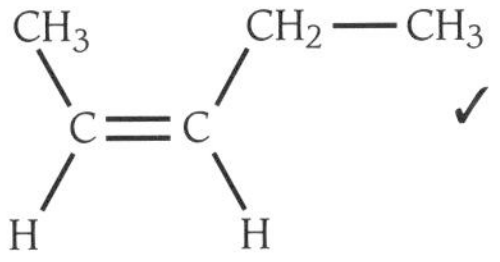

e Geometrical isomerism only occurs in compound B. All the other alkenes have two identical groups attached to the carbon atom involved in the double bond.

(vii) Cyclopentane ✓

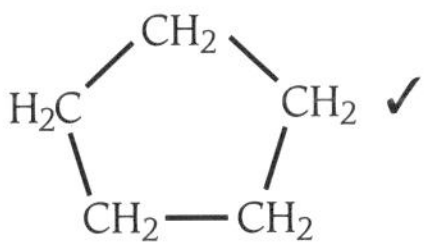

e Alkanes that are isomers of alkenes must have an empirical formula of CH_2. The only alkanes that possess this empirical formula are cyclic alkanes.

(c) The structural formulae are as follows:

(i)

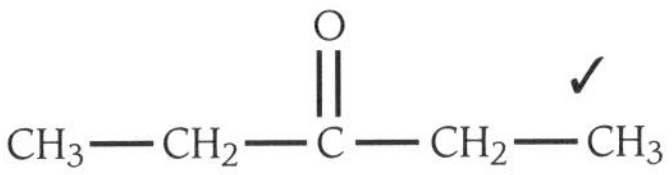

(ii) $CH_3—CH_2—CN$ ✓

(iii)

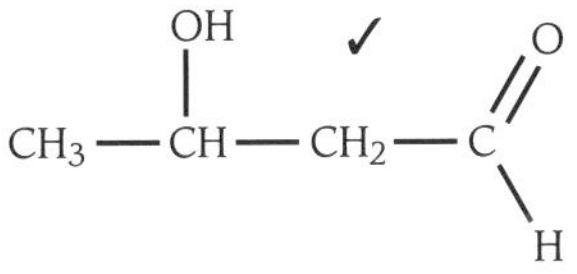

(iv)

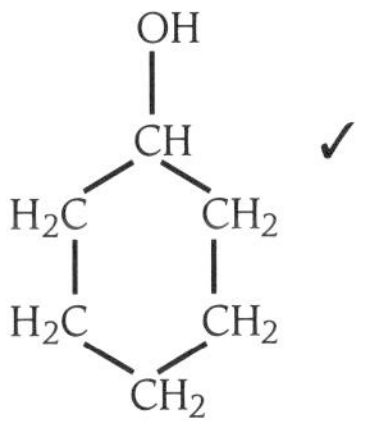

e A common mistake in part (ii) is to draw propanenitrile as $CH_3CH_2CH_2CN$. In nitriles, the C in the functional CN group is considered to be part of the hydrocarbon chain. In part (iii), the common mistake with 3-hydroxybutanal is to place the OH group on the carbon atom adjacent to the aldehyde functional group. The aldehyde group is attached to carbon number 1, so the OH group must be placed on the third carbon away from the aldehyde group. In part (iv), the prefix cyclo- means the compound is a cyclic structure and the structure could be represented as shown below.

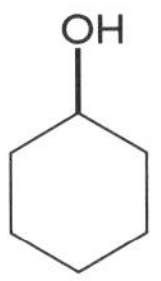

Petroleum and alkanes

(2) Consider the three fractions obtained from the fractional distillation of crude oil: *kerosine, petrol, fuel oil.*

(a) (i) Which fraction is used in jet fuel? (1 mark)

(ii) Which fraction contains the smallest molecules? (1 mark)

(iii) Which fraction is extracted at the lowest point in the fractionating column? (1 mark)

(iv) An alkane present in the kerosine fraction has a relative molecular mass of 198. This long-chain alkane undergoes thermal cracking to produce octane, C_8H_{18} and propene, C_3H_6.

- **Deduce the formula of the alkane.** (1 mark)
- **Write an equation for the cracking reaction.** (1 mark)
- **Name the type of mechanism involved in thermal cracking.** (1 mark)

(b) Octane, C_8H_{18}, is a major constituent of the petrol fraction. Explain, with the aid of equations, how the combustion of octane in the internal combustion engine leads to the formation of the pollutant gases carbon monoxide and nitrogen monoxide. Explain, with equations, how a catalytic converter removes these two pollutant gases from the exhaust pipes of car engines. (9 marks)

(c) Butane and methylpropane are isomers with the molecular formula C_4H_{10}.

(i) Draw the structures of butane and methylpropane. (2 marks)

(ii) Write an equation for the complete combustion of methylpropane. (1 mark)

(d) Butane reacts with bromine to produce 1-bromobutane.

(i) State the essential conditions for the reaction. (1 mark)

(ii) Write an overall equation for the reaction. (1 mark)

(iii) Classify the type of reaction taking place. (1 mark)

(iv) State the name and draw the structure of another mono-bromo derivative that could be formed when butane reacts with bromine. (2 marks)

(v) Write equations to describe:

- **the initiation step in the reaction** (1 mark)
- **the propagation step that leads to the formation of C_4H_9Br** (1 mark)
- **the propagation step that leads to the formation of $C_4H_8Br_2$** (1 mark)
- **the termination step that leads to the formation of C_4H_9Br** (1 mark)
- **the termination step that leads to the formation of C_8H_{18}** (1 mark)

(vi) Butane can undergo further substitution to produce a di-bromo derivative. Write an equation to show the conversion of butane into di-bromobutane. (2 marks)

Total: 30 marks

Grade-A answer to Question 2

(a) (i) Kerosine ✓

(ii) Petrol ✓

(iii) Fuel oil ✓

e At AS, you need to know the names of all the fractions, the relative order of their boiling point ranges and at least one use of each fraction. The fractions containing the largest molecules have high boiling points, so they are found at the bottom of the fractionating column, where the temperature is highest.

(iv) $C_{14}H_{30}$ ✓

e The most common mistake is to add the two formulae together, producing an alkane with the formula $C_{11}H_{24}$. However, $C_{11}H_{24}$ has an M_r of only 156. The difference between 198 and 156 is 42, which is equivalent to C_3H_6, so the formula is $C_{14}H_{30}$.

$C_{14}H_{30} \longrightarrow C_8H_{18} + 2C_3H_6$ ✓

e The equation must show the production of two propene molecules.

Free radical mechanism ✓

e Thermal cracking involves a radical mechanism, whereas catalytic cracking involves a carbocation mechanism.

(b) Octane undergoes incomplete combustion ✓ to produce carbon monoxide and water.

$C_8H_{18} + 8\frac{1}{2}O_2 \longrightarrow 8CO + 9H_2O$ ✓

The nitrogen present in the air also reacts with oxygen ✓ because the engine sparks ✓, producing the high temperature necessary to overcome the energy of activation ✓.

$N_2 + O_2 \longrightarrow 2NO$ ✓

The catalytic converter is a honeycombed ceramic structure supporting a platinum/rhodium catalyst ✓. The catalyst converts carbon monoxide to carbon dioxide ✓ and nitrogen monoxide to nitrogen gas ✓.

$2NO + 2CO \longrightarrow N_2 + 2CO_2$ ✓

The carbon monoxide is oxidised by the nitrogen monoxide ✓. Unburnt hydrocarbons also react with the nitrogen monoxide to produce carbon dioxide, nitrogen and water ✓.

$C_8H_{18} + 25NO \longrightarrow 8CO_2 + 9H_2O + 12\frac{1}{2}N_2$ ✓

e There are 13 scoring points for this section; a maximum of 9 marks can be awarded. There will be a large variation in the answers given, so the marking scheme is flexible. The last three scoring points will not be seen very often, but they must be given credit if they are seen in an exam script. It is important that you learn the equations for the production and removal of the pollutants.

(c) (i)

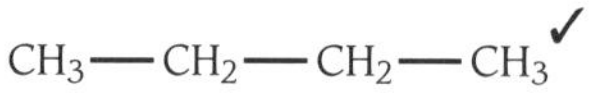

Butane

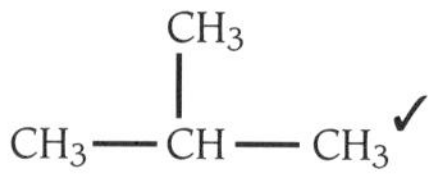

Methylpropane

The majority of candidates will draw the structures correctly.

(ii) $C_4H_{10} + 6\frac{1}{2}O_2 \longrightarrow 4CO_2 + 5H_2O$ ✓

The combustion equation is quite often incorrect. Remember, complete combustion needs oxygen and involves the production of carbon dioxide and water. If there are four carbon atoms in the hydrocarbon, then four CO_2 molecules are produced. If there are ten hydrogen atoms in the hydrocarbon, then five H_2O molecules are produced. Balance the equation by looking at the number of oxygen atoms. In this case there are 13 oxygen atoms on the right-hand side, so there must be $6\frac{1}{2}$ oxygen molecules on the left-hand side.

(d) (i) Ultraviolet light ✓

The ultraviolet light is needed to break the Br–Br bond and initiate the reaction.

(ii) $C_4H_{10} + Br_2 \longrightarrow C_4H_9Br + HBr$ ✓

An equation showing molecular formulae is acceptable in this case.

(iii) Free radical substitution ✓

The type of reaction is substitution, but it should be linked to the words 'free radical'. The answers 'electrophilic substitution' or 'nucleophilic substitution' are incorrect.

(iv) It could also produce 2-bromobutane ✓.

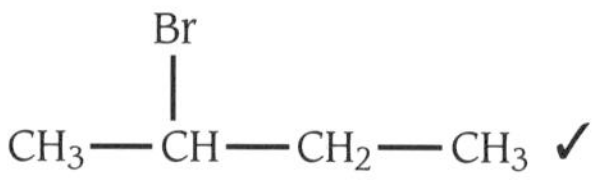

There is only one possible answer here. 3-bromobutane does not exist because it has the same structure as 2-bromobutane.

(v) $Br_2 \longrightarrow 2Br^\bullet$ ✓
$C_4H_9^\bullet + Br_2 \longrightarrow C_4H_9Br + Br^\bullet$ ✓
$C_4H_8Br^\bullet + Br_2 \longrightarrow C_4H_8Br_2 + Br^\bullet$ ✓
$C_4H_9^\bullet + Br^\bullet \longrightarrow C_4H_9Br$ ✓
$C_4H_9^\bullet + C_4H_9^\bullet \longrightarrow C_8H_{18}$ ✓

You have to know the mechanism for the chlorination of methane. However, this does not prevent the examiner setting questions involving other halogens and other alkanes, so that you have to apply your knowledge. In this case, the initiation reaction involves breaking a Br–Br bond rather than a Cl–Cl bond. The questions on propagation are the most difficult — remember that each propagation reaction involves a molecule and a radical on each side of the equation. If your equation contains hydrogen radicals, it is incorrect. The termination step involves the combination of two free radicals to produce the product specified in the question.

(vi) $C_4H_{10} + 2Br_2 \longrightarrow C_4H_8Br_2 + 2HBr$ ✓✓

This requires application of your knowledge. You know that bromination of methane produces CH_2Br_2, so it follows that bromination of C_4H_{10} produces $C_4H_8Br_2$. Remember that on introduction of each bromine atom into an alkane, one bromine molecule is used and one hydrogen bromide molecule is produced.

Alkenes

(3) (a) (i) Draw a diagram of the structural formula of propene, showing the carbon–hydrogen bonds in a way that enables you to label a bond angle of approximately 120° and a bond angle of approximately 109.5°. (3 marks)

(ii) In the reaction of propene with hydrogen bromide, write an equation for the formation of the *major product* and classify the type of reaction taking place. (3 marks)

(iii) In the reaction of propene with hydrogen bromide, draw the mechanism for the formation of the *major product* and name the final product formed. (5 marks)

(iv) In the reaction of propene with hydrogen bromide, name the *minor product* formed, draw its structural formula and explain why this is the minor product. (4 marks)

(v) Write equations and name the final product when propene reacts with:

- **bromine**
- **hydrogen at 150 °C in the presence of a nickel catalyst** (4 marks)

(vi) Write an equation describing the polymerisation of propene, name the type of polymerisation taking place and state the name of the final product. (4 marks)

(b) The compound epoxyethane (ethylene oxide) is manufactured from ethene.

(i) Write an equation for the industrial production of epoxyethane. (2 marks)

(ii) State the catalyst used in this process. (1 mark)

(iii) Some of the ethene used in the manufacture of epoxyethane is oxidised to carbon dioxide and water. Write an equation for this process. (1 mark)

(iv) State one hazard associated with the manufacture of epoxyethane. (1 mark)

(v) Explain why epoxyethane is very reactive. (1 mark)

(vi) Write an equation for the reaction of epoxyethane with one mole of water, in the presence of an acid catalyst. (1 mark)

Total: 30 marks

Grade-A answer to Question 3

(a) (i)

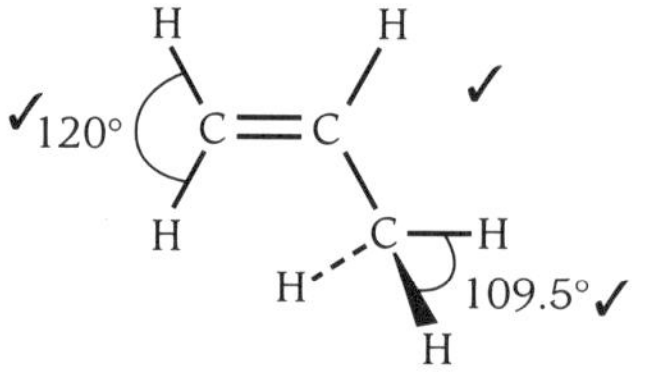

If a carbon atom has four bonds, then their distribution in space is tetrahedral and the bond angles are approximately 109.5°. If a carbon atom has three bonds (one of which is a double bond), then they are distributed in a trigonal planar fashion and the bond angles are approximately 120°. Many candidates will draw all the bonds at right angles and still achieve 3 marks by drawing the correct structure for propene and labelling any of the bond angles, shown as *x* in the diagram below, as 109.5° and any of the bond angles, shown as *y*, as 120°.

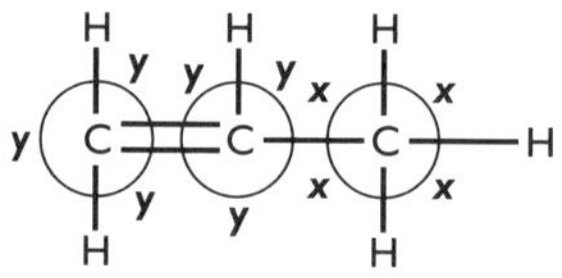

(ii) $CH_3CH{=}CH_2 + HBr \longrightarrow CH_3CHBrCH_3$ ✓✓
Electrophilic addition ✓

There is 1 mark for the balanced equation and 1 mark for the structure of the major product. The molecular equation, $C_3H_6 + HBr \longrightarrow C_3H_7Br$, would only score the equation mark because it does not show the structure of the final product.

(iii)

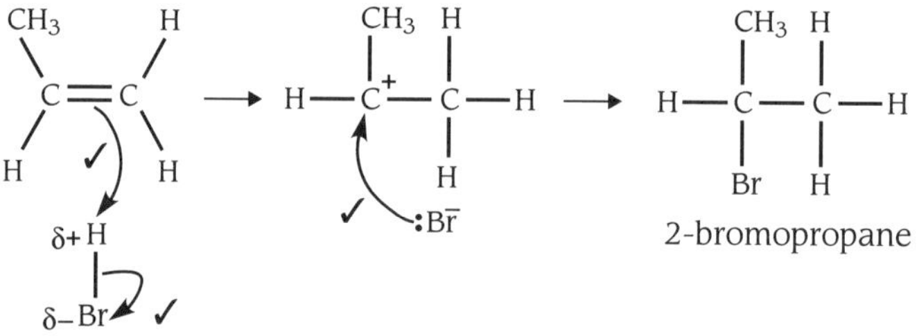

2-bromopropane ✓

There are 4 marks for the mechanism. 2 marks are for the curly arrows in the first stage of the reaction, which must be drawn accurately. There is 1 mark for the structure of the carbocation intermediate and 1 mark for the curly arrow from the bromide ion to the carbocation. It is essential that both the lone pair and the negative charge are shown on the bromide ion. The final mark is for the name of the final product. If the mechanism given is for the formation of 1-bromopropane, then 2 marks would be lost, because the name of the final product and the structure of the carbocation would be incorrect.

(iv) 1-bromopropane ✓; $CH_3CH_2CH_2Br$ ✓
The minor product is formed via a primary carbocation ✓ ($CH_3CH_2CH_2^+$) and this is less stable than the secondary carbocation ✓ ($CH_3CH^+CH_3$).

The product of the addition of an unsymmetrical reagent, for example HBr, to an unsymmetrical alkene always forms via the most stable carbocation.

(v)

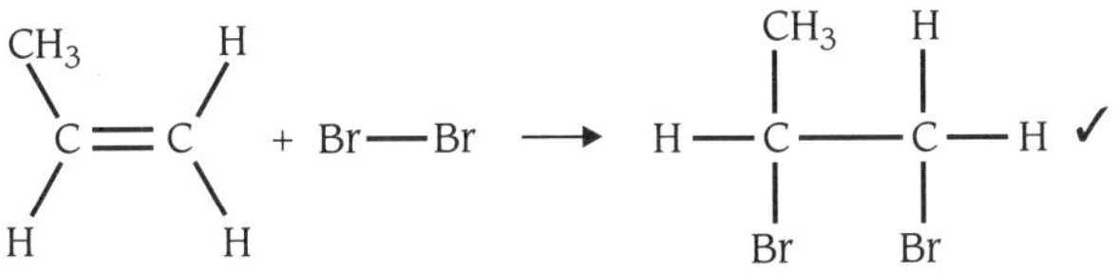

1,2-dibromopropane ✓

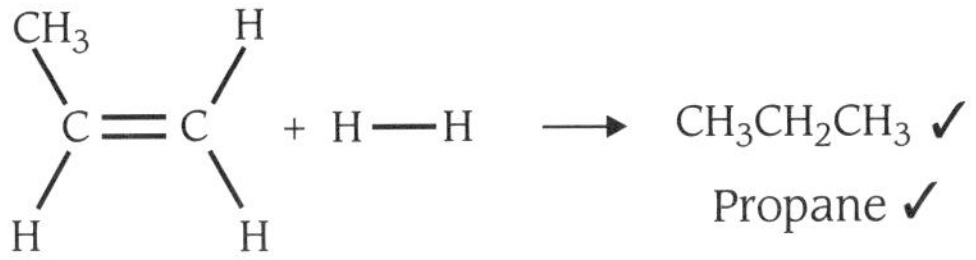

When writing these equations, always show the structure of the alkene and the structure of the final product. You should avoid writing equations that show the molecular formulae of the compounds, such as $C_3H_6 + Br_2 \longrightarrow C_3H_6Br_2$.

(vi)

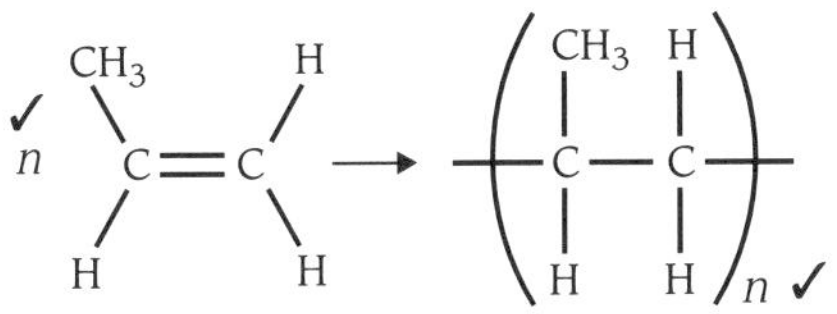

Addition polymerisation ✓
Poly(propene) ✓

A common mistake is to show the structure of the polymer as:

$$-\!\!\left(CH_3CH-CH_2\right)\!\!-_n$$

This is not acceptable because the first methyl group is not involved in the addition process. You should be linking together the two carbon atoms that are involved in the double bond. The correct repeating unit shows the methyl group coming off the main polymer chain as a side branch.

(b) (i)

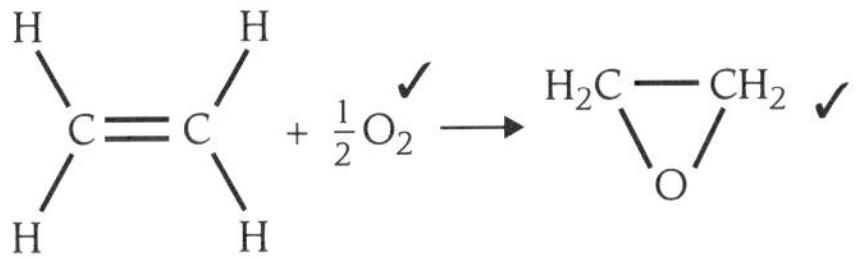

When writing this equation, you must show clearly the structure of the reactants and the products. An equation showing molecular formulae, for example C_2H_4O, is unacceptable.

(ii) Silver ✓

Silver or silver-based is acceptable.

(iii) $C_2H_4 + 3O_2 \longrightarrow 2CO_2 + 2H_2O$ ✓

Remember: in any combustion reaction, include the oxygen on the left-hand side of the equation before you try to balance it.

(iv) Ethoxyethane is potentially explosive ✓.

Other acceptable answers include: **epoxyethane is toxic** or **epoxyethane is a respiratory irritant.**

(v) It has a 3-membered ring, which is under strain and opens to accept other substituents ✓.

Other acceptable answers include: **it undergoes exothermic ring opening** or **it is susceptible to attack by nucleophiles.**

(vi) 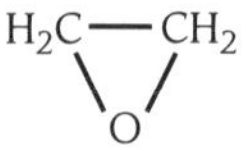
$+ H_2O \longrightarrow HO—CH_2—CH_2—OH$ ✓

You should avoid the use of molecular formulae in equations. The equation $C_2H_4O + H_2O \longrightarrow C_2H_6O_2$ is not acceptable because $C_2H_6O_2$ could represent many other possible structures.

Haloalkanes

(4) (a) (i) Explain briefly what you understand by the term *nucleophilic substitution.* (2 marks)

(ii) What features of the molecules of haloalkanes make these substances susceptible to nucleophilic substitution reactions? (2 marks)

(b) (i) State one reagent that could be used to convert 1-bromobutane into:
- **butan-1-ol**
- **pentanenitrile**
- **butylamine**

(3 marks)

(ii) Give an equation to describe the conversion of 1-bromobutane into butan-1-ol. (1 mark)

(iii) Outline a mechanism for the conversion of 1-bromobutane into pentanenitrile. (2 marks)

(c) The relative bond strength and relative bond polarity of carbon–halogen bonds are shown in the table below.

Carbon–halogen bond	Bond strength	Bond polarity
C–Cl	Stronger bond	More polar
C–Br	Weaker bond	Less polar

In an experiment to investigate the rate of hydrolysis of a haloalkane, it was found that 1-bromopropane reacted with dilute sodium hydroxide faster than 1-chloropropane.

(i) Which factor is the most important, bond strength or bond polarity, in determining the rate of hydrolysis in a haloalkane? (1 mark)

(ii) Predict the rate of hydrolysis of 1-iodopropane relative to the other two haloalkanes named above. (1 mark)

(d) (i) Write an equation for the reaction between 2-bromopropane and dilute aqueous sodium hydroxide. State the role of the hydroxide ion in this reaction, name the type of reaction taking place and outline a mechanism for the reaction. (6 marks)

(ii) Write an equation for the reaction between 2-bromopropane and ethanolic sodium hydroxide. State the role of the hydroxide ion in this reaction, name the type of reaction taking place and outline a mechanism for the reaction. (6 marks)

(e) When 2-bromo-3-methylbutane reacts with potassium hydroxide under aqueous conditions, it produces an alcohol, compound A. When the same haloalkane reacts with potassium hydroxide under alcoholic conditions it produces a mixture of two isomeric alkenes, compounds B and C. Give the structures and names of the three compounds A, B and C. (6 marks)

Total: 30 marks

Grade-A answer to Question 4

(a) (i) Nucleophilic substitution is the replacement ✓ of an atom (or group of atoms) by a nucleophile, which is an electron pair donor ✓ that attacks an electron-deficient site.

e There is 1 mark for using any word that means substitution and 1 mark for understanding the importance of the lone pair in nucleophilic attack.

(ii) Haloalkanes are susceptible to nucleophilic attack because the carbon–halogen bond is polar ✓. The nucleophile attacks the electron-deficient carbon atom ✓ and at the same time the halogen atom leaves as a halide ion.

e A mark can be scored by either a diagram showing a polar bond with the symbols $\delta+$ and $\delta-$, or by discussing the charge separation in the bond due to the differing electronegativities of the carbon and chlorine atoms. There is a mark for understanding that the lone pair of the nucleophile is attracted to the $\delta+$ on the carbon atom.

(b) (i) Sodium hydroxide (NaOH) ✓
Potassium cyanide (KCN) ✓
Ammonia (NH_3) ✓

e **Potassium hydroxide** is an alternative to sodium hydroxide. **Sodium cyanide** is an alternative to potassium cyanide. Ammonia is the only acceptable answer to the last part. A common mistake is to use hydrogen cyanide (HCN) instead of KCN or NaCN.

(ii) $CH_3CH_2CH_2CH_2Br + NaOH \longrightarrow CH_3CH_2CH_2CH_2OH + NaBr$ ✓

You need to use structural formulae for the two organic compounds to show that the substitution has taken place in the 1-position. No marks are awarded for the use of the molecular formulae C_4H_9Br and C_4H_9OH.

(iii)

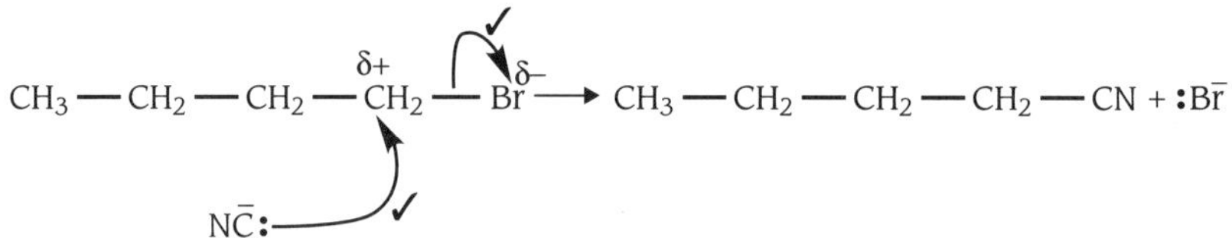

The number of marks allocated to nucleophilic substitution mechanisms is 2 or 3. In this case, 2 marks are allocated, for the correct positioning of the curly arrows. However, there could have been a third mark for the structure of the products. It is important that you include the cyanide ion in the mechanism and not the reagent, NaCN.

(c) (i) Bond strength is the more important factor ✓.

This question could be presented using numerical data, but always remember that bond strength is the most important factor.

(ii) 1-iodopropane reacts more quickly ✓ than the other two haloalkanes because it has the weakest carbon–halogen bond.

You need to be able to use information from unfamiliar situations to predict the rate of hydrolysis of haloalkanes. An alternative question would be to predict the rate of hydrolysis of 1-fluoropropane, which would react more slowly because the C–F bond is the strongest.

(d) (i) $CH_3CHBrCH_3 + NaOH \longrightarrow CH_3CH(OH)CH_3 + NaBr$ ✓
The OH^- ion is acting as a nucleophile ✓ because it donates an electron pair. The reaction type is nucleophilic substitution ✓. The mechanism for the reaction is outlined below:

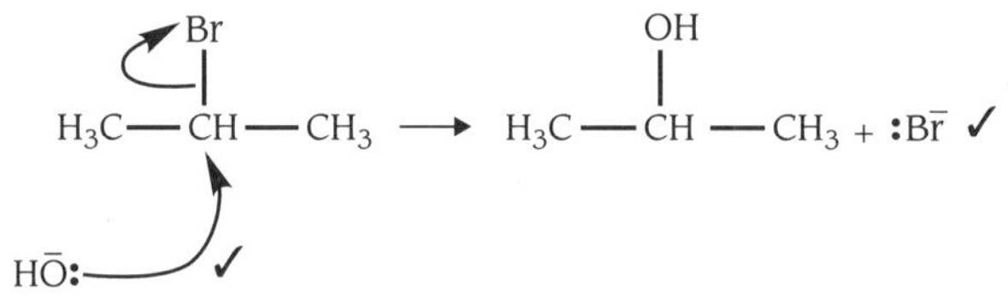

The equation must be balanced and contain the reagent NaOH. **Hydrolysis** is an alternative answer to nucleophilic substitution. The mechanism has been allocated 3 marks because the product of the reaction is not given in the question. Although 2-bromopropane is a secondary haloalkane, it undergoes nucleophilic substitution in exactly the same way as a primary haloalkane. There are 2 marks for correct positioning of the curly products and 1 mark for the final products.

(ii) $CH_3CHBrCH_3 + NaOH \longrightarrow CH_3CH{=}CH_2 + NaBr + H_2O$ ✓
The OH^- ion is acting as a base ✓ by accepting a proton, H^+, from the haloalkane. The reaction type is elimination ✓. The mechanism for the reaction is outlined below:

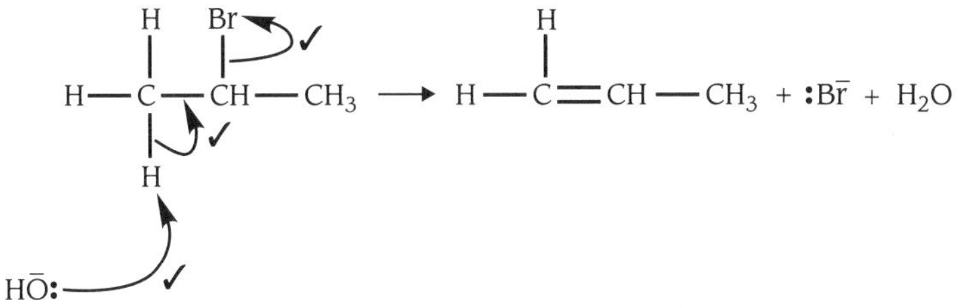

The equation must be balanced and contain the reagent NaOH. There are *no alternative answers* to **base** and **elimination**. It is essential that the curly arrows are in the correct place for 3 marks to be scored in the mechanism.

(e)

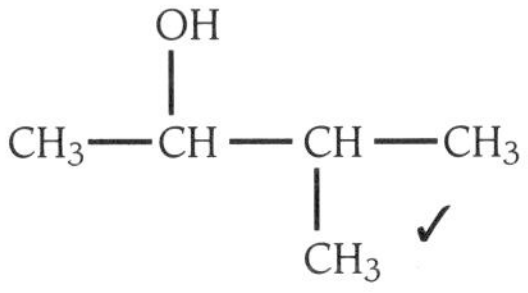

Compound A:
3-methylbutan-2-ol ✓

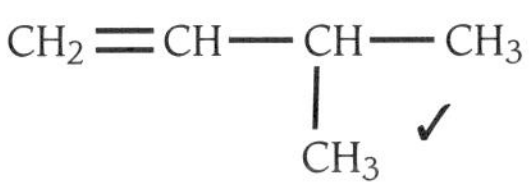

Compound B:
3-methylbut-1-ene ✓

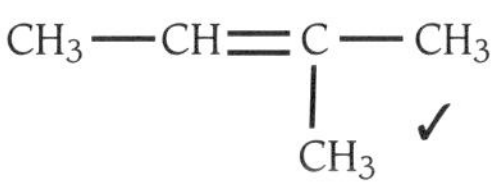

Compound C:
2-methylbut-2-ene ✓

There is 1 mark for each correct name and 1 mark for each correct structure.

Alcohols

(5) There are four isomeric alcohols with the molecular formula $C_4H_{10}O$.

(a) Draw the structures and state the names of the four isomeric alcohols with the molecular formula $C_4H_{10}O$. (8 marks)

(b) Classify each alcohol as primary, secondary or tertiary. (4 marks)

(c) State the reagent needed for the oxidation of these alcohols. (1 mark)

(d) Write equations to describe the oxidation of each alcohol under *reflux* conditions and name the product formed in each reaction. If the alcohol cannot be oxidised, then state 'no reaction'. (7 marks)

(e) Write an equation to describe the oxidation of *one* of the *primary* alcohols under *distillation* conditions and name the product formed. (2 marks)

(f) Write an equation, then draw the mechanism, for the dehydration of the *tertiary* alcohol when it is warmed with concentrated sulphuric acid at 180°C. (5 marks)

(g) Two compounds that can be obtained by the oxidation of alcohols are shown below:

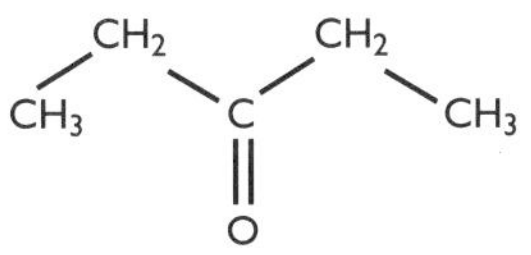

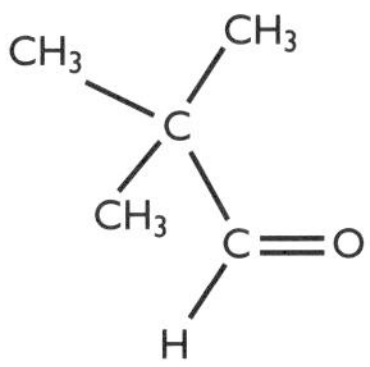

Describe a simple test that will enable you to distinguish between these two compounds. (3 marks)

Total: 30 marks

Grade-A answer to Question 5

(a)

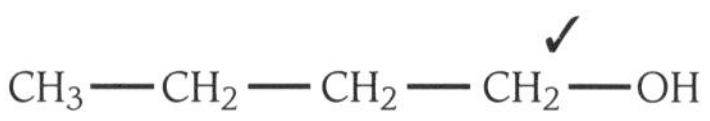

Butan-1-ol ✓

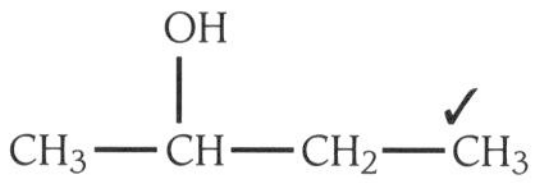

Butan-2-ol ✓

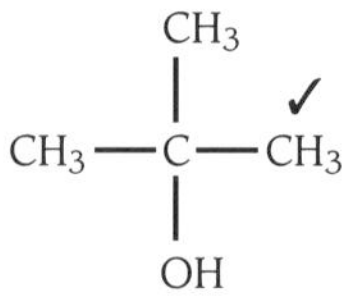

2-methylpropan-2-ol ✓

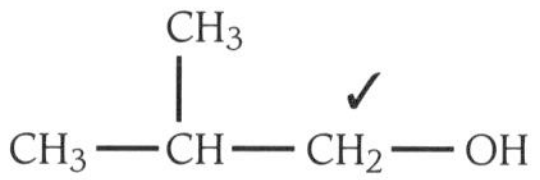

2-methylpropan-1-ol ✓

Methylpropan-2-ol and **methylpropan-1-ol** are acceptable answers for the third and fourth isomers.

(b) Butan-1-ol is primary ✓; butan-2-ol is secondary ✓; 2-methylpropan-2-ol is tertiary ✓; 2-methylpropan-1-ol is primary ✓.

A common mistake is to classify 2-methylpropan-1-ol as a tertiary alcohol.

(c) Acidified potassium dichromate(VI) ✓

Either the word **acidified** or **with dilute sulphuric acid** *must* be present for the mark to be awarded for potassium dichromate(VI). The formula $\mathbf{K_2Cr_2O_7}$, rather than the name, would also be acceptable. Alternative answers include **acidified** $\mathbf{Na_2Cr_2O_7}$ and **acidified** $\mathbf{KMnO_4}$.

(d) $CH_3CH_2CH_2CH_2OH + 2[O] \longrightarrow CH_3CH_2CH_2COOH + H_2O$ ✓; butanoic acid ✓
$CH_3CH(OH)CH_2CH_3 + H_2O \longrightarrow CH_3COCH_2CH_3 + H_2O$ ✓; butanone ✓
$(CH_3)_2CHCH_2OH + 2[O] \longrightarrow (CH_3)_2CHCOOH + H_2O$ ✓; methylpropanoic acid ✓
$(CH_3)_3COH$ is a tertiary alcohol and so is resistant to oxidation ✓.

The symbol [O] is used to simplify the equations for the oxidation of alcohols. When primary alcohols are oxidised under reflux condition they produce carboxylic acids. When secondary alcohols are oxidised they produce ketones. Tertiary alcohols are resistant to oxidation. Butan-2-one is not an acceptable answer for the name of the ketone because the number is not required. 2-methylpropanoic acid is an acceptable alternative to methylpropanoic acid.

(e) $CH_3CH_2CH_2CH_2OH + [O] \longrightarrow CH_3CH_2CH_2CHO + H_2O$ ✓; butanal ✓

Primary alcohols are oxidised to aldehydes under distillation conditions. The full structure of the aldehyde should be shown in the equation — C_4H_8O is not an acceptable answer.

(f)

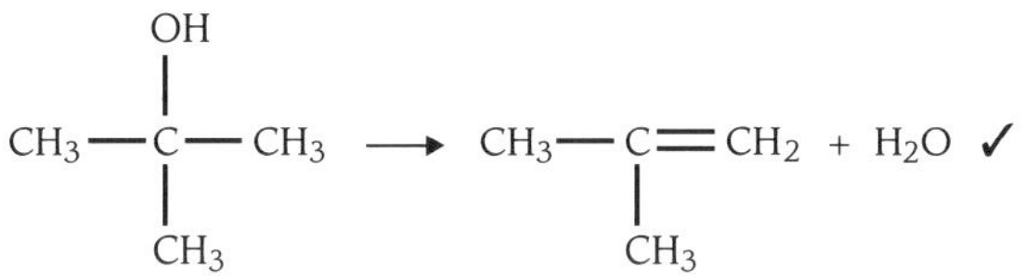

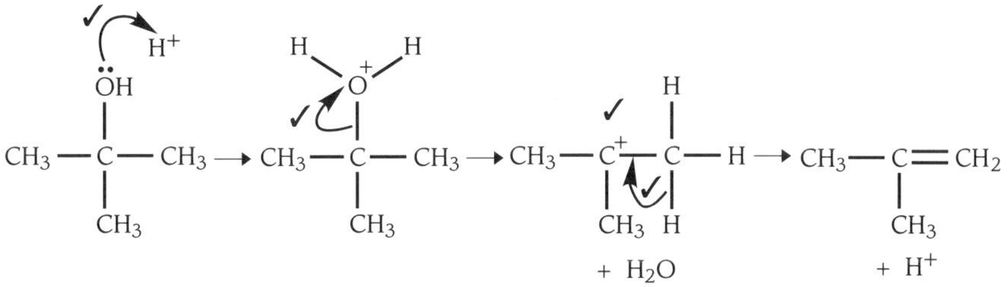

The equation should *not* include H_2SO_4, unless it appears on both sides. The equation must be balanced. The full structure of the alkene (not C_4H_8) should be shown in the equation. There are 4 marks for the mechanism. There is 1 mark for the lone pair on the oxygen of the OH group and 1 mark for a correctly positioned curly arrow with a positive charge on the oxygen. There is a mark for the structure of the intermediate carbocation. The final mark is for the curly arrow showing the formation of the double bond.

(g) Add Fehling's solution ✓.The ketone ($CH_3CH_2COCH_2CH_3$) does not react ✓. The aldehyde ($(CH_3)_3CCHO$) gives a red precipitate ✓.

There are alternative answers. **Add Tollen's reagent ✓ (or ammoniacal silver nitrate) — the aldehyde gives a silver mirror ✓ whereas the ketone does not react ✓** or **add acidified $K_2Cr_2O_7$ ✓ — the aldehyde changes the colour of the solution from orange to green ✓ whereas the ketone gives no reaction ✓.**

Nomenclature and isomerism

(1) (a) Draw and name the four structural isomers of C_4H_9Br. (8 marks)

(b) An organic compound contains 54.55% carbon, 9.09% hydrogen and 36.36% oxygen by mass. It has a relative molecular mass of 88.

(i) Calculate the empirical formula of the compound. (3 marks)

(ii) Deduce the molecular formula of the compound. (1 mark)

(iii) Draw and name two isomeric carboxylic acids that have this molecular formula. (4 marks)

(c) Consider the six organic compounds shown below:

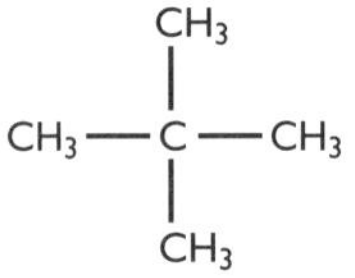

Compound A

$$CH_3-CH=CH-CH_3$$

Compound B

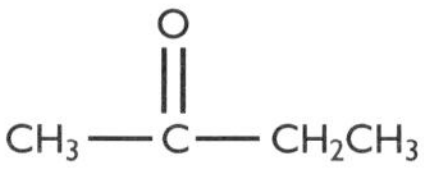

Compound C

$$H_2C=CH-CH_2-CH_3$$

Compound D

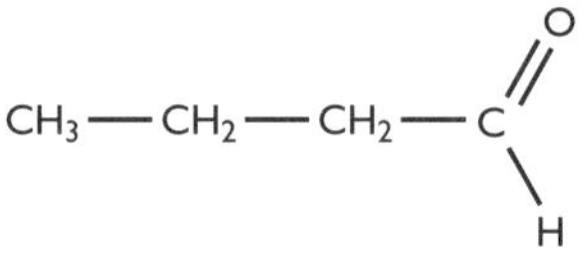

Compound E

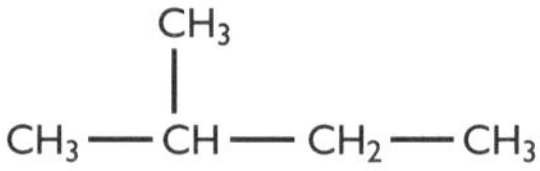

Compound F

(i) Name the compounds labelled A to F. (6 marks)

(ii) Using the letters A to F, identify a pair of isomers that exhibit:

- **chain isomerism**
- **position isomerism**
- **functional group isomerism** (3 marks)

(d) The structure of butenedioic acid is shown below:

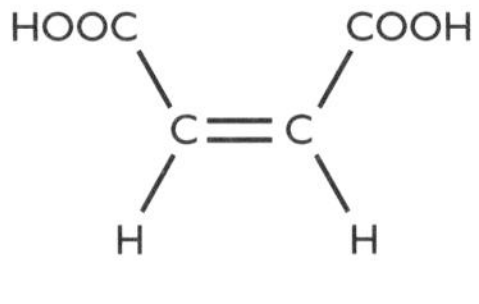

(i) Explain why butenedioic acid is capable of exhibiting geometrical isomerism. (2 marks)

(ii) Draw the other geometrical isomer of butenedioic acid. (1 mark)

(e) The structure of the ether ethoxyethane is shown below:

$$CH_3-CH_2-O-CH_2-CH_3$$

Draw and name the structure of an isomer of ethoxyethane that has a much higher boiling point than the ether. (2 marks)

Total: 30 marks

Grade-A answer to Question 1

(a) The four structural isomers are shown below.

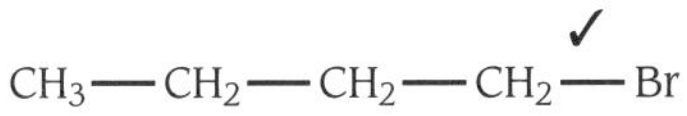

1-bromobutane ✓

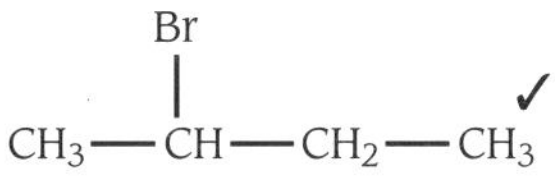

2-bromobutane ✓

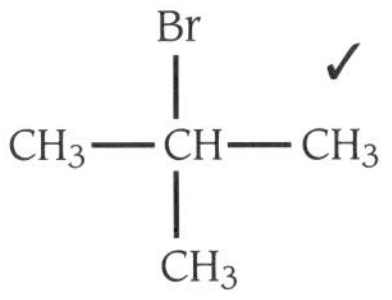

2-bromo-2-methylpropane ✓

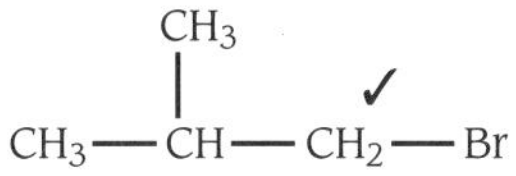

1-bromo-2-methylpropane ✓

2-bromomethylpropane and **1-bromomethylpropane** are acceptable answers for 2-bromo-2-methylpropane and 1-bromo-2-methylpropane respectively.

(b) (i)

	Carbon	Hydrogen	Oxygen
$\frac{m}{M}$	$\frac{54.55\%}{12}$	$\frac{9.09\%}{1}$	$\frac{36.36\%}{16}$
Moles	4.54	9.09	2.27 ✓
Ratio	2	4	1 ✓

Empirical formula is C_2H_4O ✓

The correct empirical formula gains 3 marks. However, it is important to show your working out so that consequential marks can be awarded if you make a careless arithmetical error.

(ii) $C_2H_4O = 44$. Therefore, if the M_r is 88, the molecular formula is $C_4H_8O_2$ ✓.

The atoms can be given in any order to gain the mark but it is usual in molecular formulae to state the elements in the order carbon, hydrogen, oxygen.

(iii) The two carboxylic acids are:

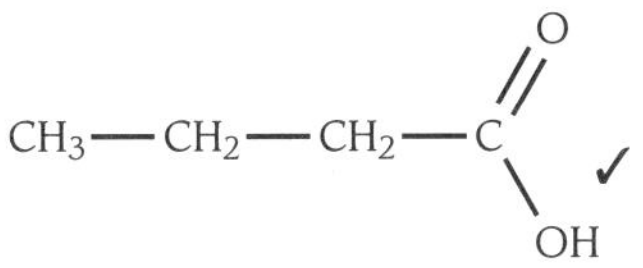

Butanoic acid ✓

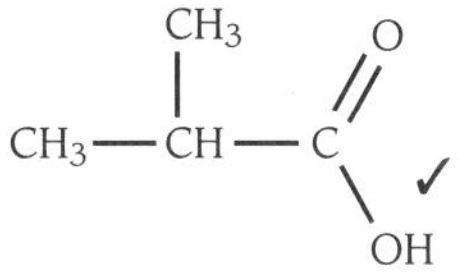

2-methylpropanoic acid ✓

The properties of carboxylic acids are not covered in this module. However, their nomenclature needs to be studied because they are products of the oxidation of primary alcohols. **Methylpropanoic acid** is an acceptable name for the branched isomer.

(c) (i) A = 2,2-dimethylpropane ✓; B = but-2-ene ✓; C = butanone ✓; D = but-1-ene ✓; E = butanal ✓; F = 2-methylbutane ✓

e Compound A could be named **dimethylpropane**; compound F could be named **methylbutane**. However, the numbers are essential in the alkenes, compounds B and D. It is essential that no numbers are included in the names of compounds C and E.

(ii) Compounds A and F exhibit chain isomerism ✓.
Compounds B and D exhibit position isomerism ✓.
Compounds C and E exhibit functional group isomerism ✓.

e Chain isomerism occurs when there are two or more ways of arranging the carbon skeleton in the molecule. Position isomerism occurs when the functional group is joined at different places on the carbon skeleton (in this case the double bond). Functional group isomerism occurs when the two compounds have the same molecular formula but have the functional group in a different position.

(d) (i) It contains a double bond ✓ which cannot rotate ✓.

e The isomer shown in the question is the *cis*-isomer. The other geometrical isomer is the *trans*-isomer.

(ii)

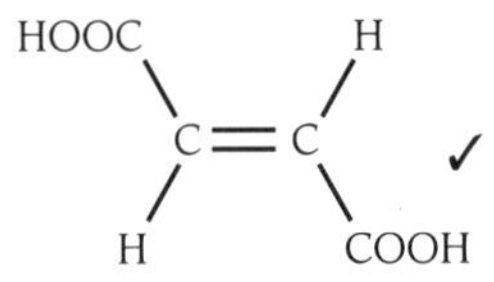

(e) $CH_3CH_2CH_2CH_2OH$ ✓
Butan-1-ol ✓

e Any alcohol containing four carbon atoms is acceptable. There is 1 mark for the structure and 1 mark for the name associated with that structure. Other alternative answers include **butan-2-ol, 2-methylpropan-2-ol** and **2-methylpropan-1-ol**. All these alcohols have a higher boiling point than the ether because they all have stronger intermolecular forces (H-bonding), due to the presence of the OH group.

Petroleum and alkanes

(2) (a) Propane reacts with chlorine to produce two possible mono-chloro derivatives.

(i) Draw and name the two possible mono-chloro derivatives. (4 marks)

(ii) State the essential conditions for the chlorination of propane. (1 mark)

(iii) Using *molecular* formulae, write an overall equation for the conversion of propane into one of the chloropropane derivatives. (2 marks)

(iv) For the conversion of propane into chloropropane, write an equation for
- **the initiation step**
- ***two* propagation steps**
- **the termination step that leads to the formation of C_6H_{14}** (4 marks)

(v) **Propane can undergo disubstitution when it reacts with chlorine. Write an equation for the conversion of propane into dichloropropane. Suggest structures for all the possible dichloro derivatives.** (6 marks)

(b) Petrol is a fraction obtained from crude oil. Molecules with the molecular formula C_8H_{18} are present in the petrol fraction.

(i) **State the method used to separate the petrol fraction from the other fractions in crude oil.** (1 mark)

(ii) **Explain why it is possible to separate petrol from the other fractions in crude oil.** (1 mark)

(iii) **Write an equation for the complete combustion of C_8H_{18}.** (2 marks)

(iv) **Draw and name the structural isomer of C_8H_{18} that has the *lowest* boiling point.** (2 marks)

(v) **How many possible mono-chloro derivatives are formed when the isomer in part (iv) reacts with chlorine in UV light. Briefly explain your answer.** (2 marks)

(vi) **C_8H_{18} can be formed from the cracking of $C_{14}H_{30}$. There is only one other product in the cracking process. Write an equation to describe this cracking process.** (1 mark)

(vii) **The cracking in part (vi) is carried out in the presence of a zeolite catalyst at a temperature of 450 °C. What type of reactive intermediate is formed?** (1 mark)

(viii) **$C_{14}H_{30}$ can also be thermally cracked at 850 °C to give a mixture of propene and ethene in a 2:1 ratio and an alkane. Write an equation to describe this process, state the type of bond fission occurring during the reaction and give the type of reactive intermediate formed during the mechanism.** (3 marks)

Total: 30 marks

Grade-A answer to Question 2

(a) (i) The two mono-chloro derivatives formed are:

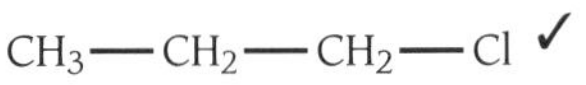

1-chloropropane ✓

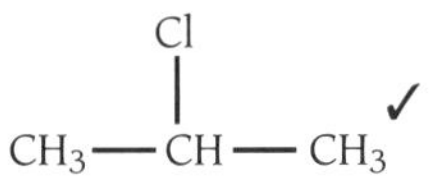

2-chloropropane ✓

e Chlorination of methane produces chloromethane. Chlorination of propane produces two products because there are two different types of hydrogen that can be replaced in the propane molecule. 3-chloropropane does not exist because it is the same as 1-chloropropane.

(ii) UV light ✓

e The ultraviolet light is needed to break the Cl–Cl bond and initiate the reaction.

(iii) $C_3H_8 + Cl_2 \longrightarrow C_3H_7Cl + HCl$ ✓✓

There is 1 mark for the formula of chloropropane and 1 mark for the balanced equation. Remember, when you introduce a chlorine atom into an alkane, a chlorine molecule is used and hydrogen chloride is one of the products.

(iv) $Cl_2 \longrightarrow 2Cl\bullet$ ✓
$C_3H_8 + Cl\bullet \longrightarrow C_3H_7\bullet + HCl$ ✓
$C_3H_7\bullet + Cl_2 \longrightarrow C_3H_7Cl + Cl\bullet$ ✓
$C_3H_7\bullet + C_3H_7\bullet \longrightarrow C_6H_{14}$ ✓

There is only one possible answer for the initiation step. For the two propagation steps the most common answers are given. However, there are alternatives: a molecule and a radical must react correctly to produce another molecule and a radical. There is only one possible answer for the termination step specified.

(v) $C_3H_8 + 2Cl_2 \longrightarrow C_3H_6Cl_2 + 2HCl$ ✓✓

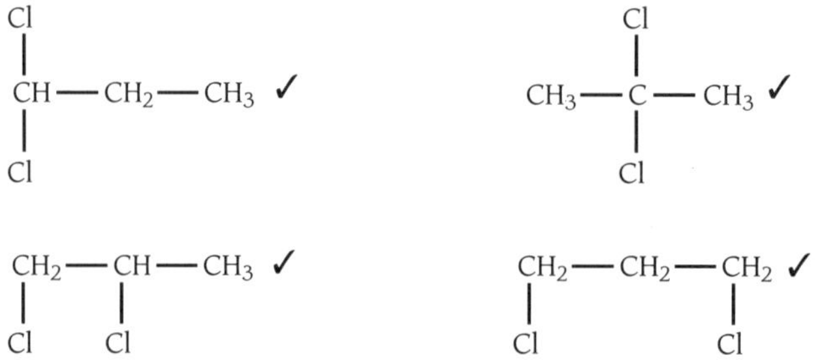

Methane reacts further with chlorine to produce dichloromethane. You should be able to predict that propane will react similarly with chlorine to produce dichloropropane. There are four possible dichloropropane derivatives. If you wrote down more than these four structures the examiner would use the list principle to mark your work: five structures means there must be at least one incorrect structure, so you score a maximum 3 marks out of 4; six structures means that there must be at least two incorrect structures, so you score a maximum of 2 marks.

(b) (i) Fractional distillation ✓

Distillation alone would not score the mark.

(ii) Each fraction has a different boiling point range ✓ because it contains molecules of a certain size.

The separation of crude oil is achieved because the molecules have different sizes, so they have different intermolecular forces and therefore different boiling points.

(iii) $C_8H_{18} + 12\frac{1}{2}O_2 \longrightarrow 8CO_2 + 9H_2O$ ✓✓

There is 1 mark is for the production of CO_2 and H_2O and 1 mark for a balanced equation.

(iv)

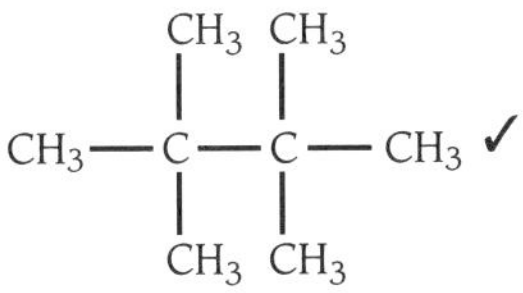

2,2,3,3,-tetramethylbutane ✓

The most branched isomer of C_8H_{18} has the lowest boiling point because it has the lowest surface area and the weakest van der Waals forces. There is 1 mark for the structure and 1 mark for the name — tetramethylbutane being acceptable.

(v) Only one ✓ monochloro derivative forms. The molecule is totally symmetrical. All the hydrogen atoms in the molecule are in identical ✓ environments. Therefore, whichever hydrogen atom is replaced, the same product is formed.

In methane, there is only one monochloro derivative because all the hydrogen atoms are identical. This question involves application of knowledge, which many candidates find difficult.

(vi) $C_{14}H_{30} \longrightarrow C_8H_{18} + C_6H_{12}$ ✓

Alternatives to C_6H_{12} are $2C_3H_6$ or $3C_2H_4$.

(vii) Carbocations ✓

Catalytic cracking is carried out at lower temperatures than thermal cracking and the intermediates formed are called carbocations.

(viii) $C_{14}H_{30} \longrightarrow C_6H_{14} + 2C_3H_6 + C_2H_4$ ✓
Homolytic bond fission ✓; free radical ✓

The reactant and two of the products are given, so the mark is for identifying C_6H_{14} and placing it in a balanced equation. Remember to check that the equation is balanced. At high temperatures, the C–C and C–H bonds split by homolytic bond fission to produce free radicals.

Alkenes

(3) (a) The structures of three alkenes are shown below.

Compound A

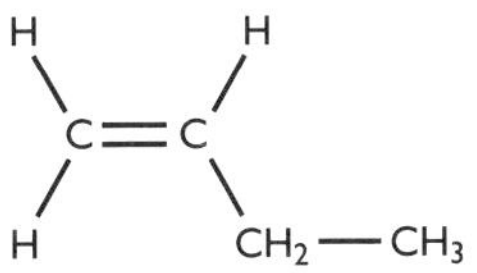

Compound B

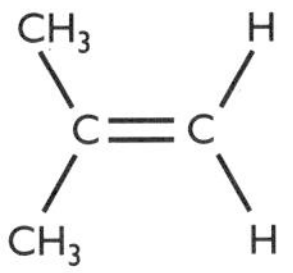

Compound C

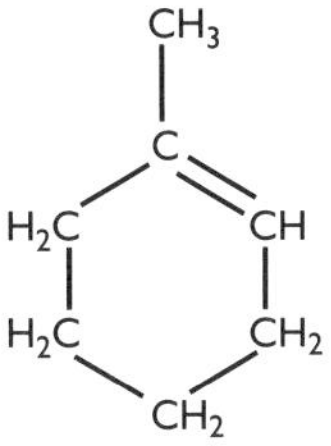

(i) **Name compounds A and B.** (2 marks)

(ii) **Describe a simple test to confirm the presence of the carbon–carbon double bond in all three compounds.** (2 marks)

(iii) **Write an equation to show the formation of the major product when compound A reacts with HBr. Name the major product formed in this reaction.** (2 marks)

(iv) **State the name of compound B and draw the mechanism for its reaction with concentrated sulphuric acid to produce the major product.** (5 marks)

(v) **Predict the major product when compound C reacts with HBr and explain, in terms of the stability of the intermediate carbocations, *why* this is the major product.** (3 marks)

(vi) **Write equations to describe:**

- **the polymerisation of compound A**
- **the reaction of compound B with bromine**
- **the reaction of compound C when it is heated with hydrogen in the presence of a nickel catalyst** (6 marks)

(b) Epoxyethane undergoes hydration with excess water to produce ethane-1,2-diol. If the proportion of water is lowered, more complex polymeric products are formed. Epoxyethane also reacts with other nucleophiles, such as alcohols and ammonia.

(i) **Draw the structure of ethane-1,2-diol and give *two* uses of this compound.** (3 marks)

(ii) **Write an equation to describe the polymerisation of epoxyethane with water.** (2 marks)

(iii) **Write an equation for the reaction of epoxyethane with propan-1-ol.** (2 marks)

(iv) **State *two* uses of the polymeric products formed when epoxyethane reacts with alcohols.** (2 marks)

(v) **Predict the structure of the product formed when epoxyethane reacts with ammonia.** (1 mark)

Total: 30 marks

■ ■ ■

Grade-A answer to Question 3

(a) (i) Compound A is but-1-ene ✓; compound B is 2-methylpropene ✓.

Methylpropene is an acceptable answer for compound B.

(ii) Add bromine ✓; the bromine is decolourised ✓.

Adding bromine is the commonest test for unsaturation, but others do exist. Avoid using the decolourisation of potassium manganate(VII) as an alternative test because other reagents, such as primary and secondary alcohols and aldehydes, also decolourise it in acidic conditions.

(iii) $CH_2{=}CHCH_2CH_3 + HBr \longrightarrow CH_3CHBrCH_2CH_3$ ✓
The major product is 2-bromobutane ✓.

The equation for the formation of 1-bromobutane would earn 1 mark but the second mark would be lost because of the incorrect major product name.

(iv) Electrophilic addition ✓

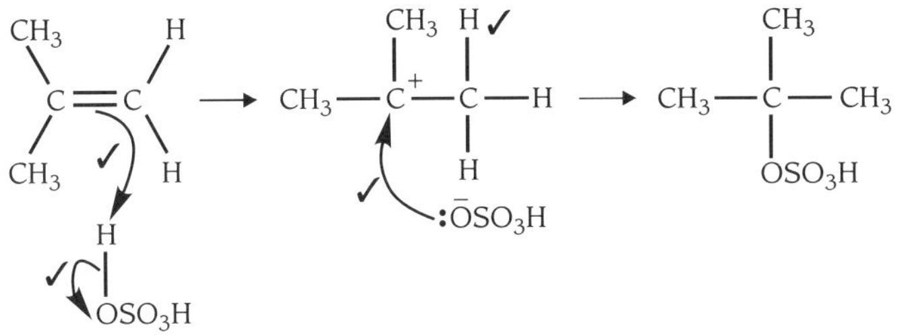

Both 'electrophilic' and 'addition' are needed to gain the first mark. If you have shown the formation of the wrong product, i.e. $(CH_3)_2CHCH_2OSO_3H$, then you can only score 2 of the 4 marks available for the mechanism.

(v) The major product always forms via the most stable carbocation. In this case, the tertiary carbocation ✓ is more stable than the secondary carbocation ✓. The final product has the structure shown below.

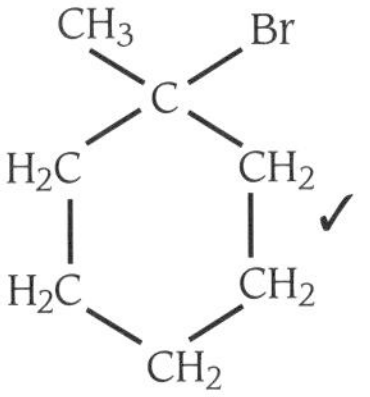

It is important when discussing carbocation stability that you identify the correct ones for this mechanism. This reaction involves a tertiary and a secondary carbocation but other reactions could involve a primary carbocation.

(vi) The equation for the polymerisation of compound A is shown below.

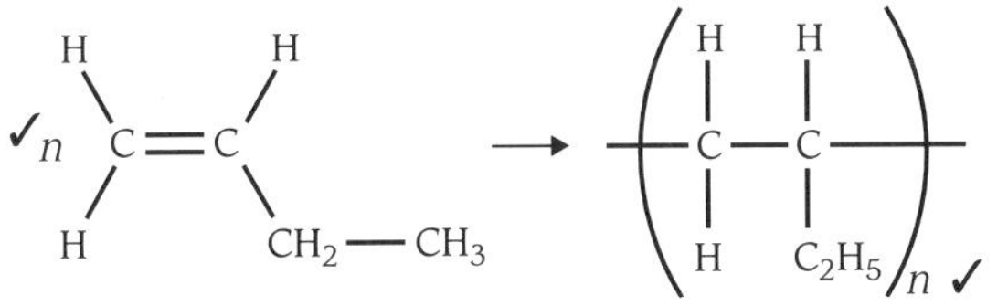

The equation for the reaction of compound B with bromine is shown below.

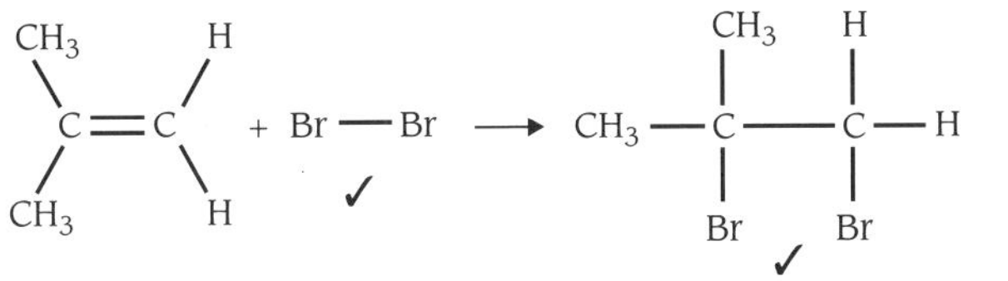

The equation for the reaction of compound C heated with hydrogen in the presence of a nickel catalyst is shown below.

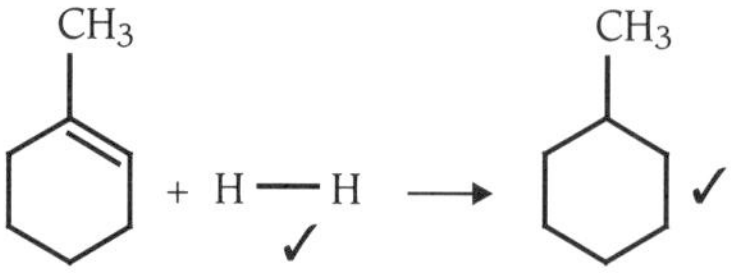

In each case, there is 1 mark for a balanced equation and 1 mark for the correct structure of the product.

(b) (i) $HOCH_2CH_2OH$ ✓

Two uses are antifreeze ✓ and polyester production ✓.

The **preparation of terylene** is an alternative answer to the preparation of polyesters. These two uses of diols are stated in the specification.

(ii)

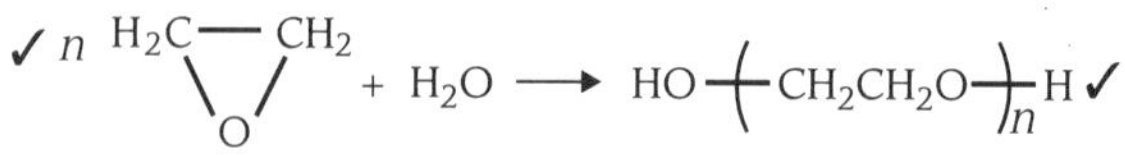

There is 1 mark for the final product and 1 mark for the equation. It is important to include the symbol 'n' on both sides of the equation.

(iii)

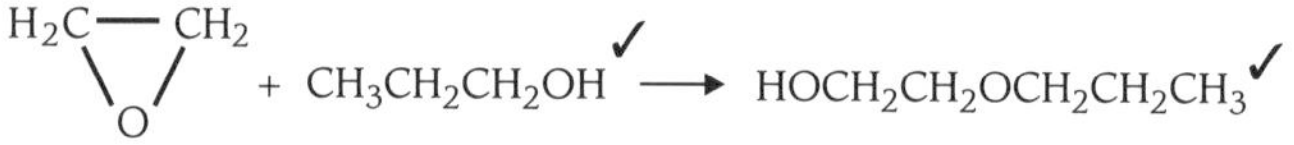

You need to develop a system to predict the reaction of epoxyethane with nucleophiles.

- If the nucleophile is water or an alcohol, it contains an OH group.
- Attach the H from this OH group to the oxygen in the epoxyethane, which now looks like this:

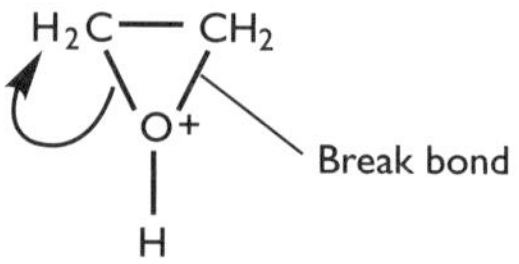

- Swivel the OH group to the left and break the C–O bond on the right.
- Now attach the other part of the nucleophile to the carbon on the right.
- Remember: the connection is always from the oxygen atom in water and alcohols and always from the nitrogen in ammonia.

The structure of the final product, with the added atoms in bold, is:

$HOCH_2CH_2\mathbf{OCH_2CH_2CH_3}$

(iv) They are used as solvents ✓ and in printing inks ✓.

This is always a low-scoring question and many candidates will not score 2 marks. Alternative answers include **brake fluids** and **plasticisers**.

(v) $HOCH_2CH_2NH_2$ ✓

Using a similar method to the one explained in part (iii), the H goes to the left and the rest of the ammonia joins through the N. The structure of the final product, with the added atoms in bold, is:

$HOCH_2CH_2\mathbf{NH_2}$

Haloalkanes

(4) (a) (i) Write a balanced equation for the reaction between 1-bromopropane and ammonia. (2 marks)

(ii) Classify ammonia as either a nucleophile or an electrophile and justify your answer. (2 marks)

(iii) Outline a mechanism for the reaction between 1-bromopropane and ammonia. (4 marks)

(b) Suggest the structure of the haloalkane that could be used to form the compound hexane-1,6-diamine ($H_2NCH_2CH_2CH_2CH_2CH_2CH_2NH_2$). Write an equation for the conversion of the haloalkane into the diamine. (3 marks)

(c) Compound P of molecular formula C_4H_8 is an alkene capable of exhibiting geometrical isomerism. It reacts with HBr to produce compound Q of molecular formula C_4H_9Br. Compound Q reacts with aqueous sodium hydroxide to produce compound R, $C_4H_{10}O$. Compound Q also reacts with sodium cyanide in a solvent of ethanol to produce compound S, C_5H_9N. Compound S is converted to compound T, $C_5H_{10}O_2$, by boiling in dilute hydrochloric acid.

(i) Give the structural formulae and the names of the compounds P, Q, R, S and T. (10 marks)

(ii) State the type of mechanism occurring in the conversion of P to Q and in the conversion of Q to R. (2 marks)

(iii) Outline the mechanism for the conversion of Q to S. (3 marks)

(d) Predict the structures of the organic compounds A to D, produced when the haloalkanes shown below react with potassium hydroxide. (4 marks)

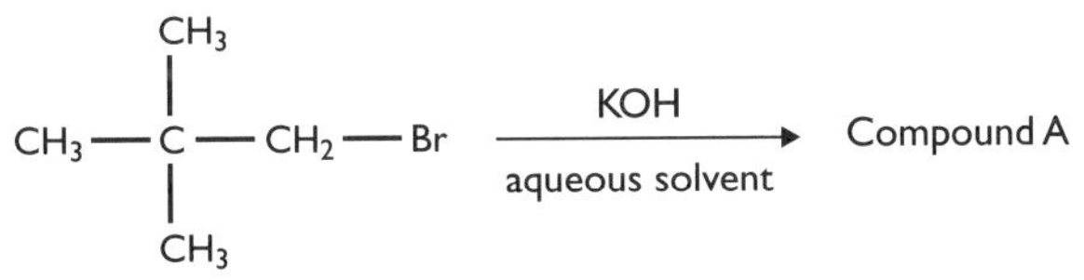

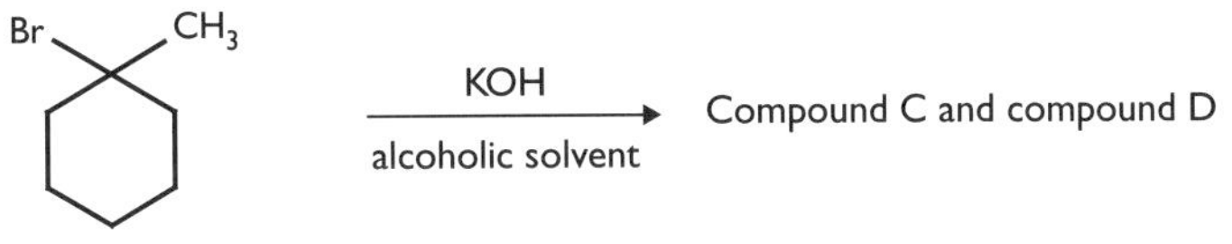

Total: 30 marks

Grade-A answer to Question 4

(a) (i) $CH_3CH_2CH_2Br + 2NH_3 \longrightarrow CH_3CH_2CH_2NH_2 + NH_4Br$ ✓✓

$CH_3CH_2CH_2Br + NH_3 \longrightarrow CH_3CH_2CH_2NH_2 + HBr$, would score just 1 mark.

(ii) Ammonia is a nucleophile ✓ because it donates an electron pair ✓.

Lewis base is an alternative answer to nucleophile.

(iii) The mechanism for the reaction of 1-bromopropane and ammonia is shown below.

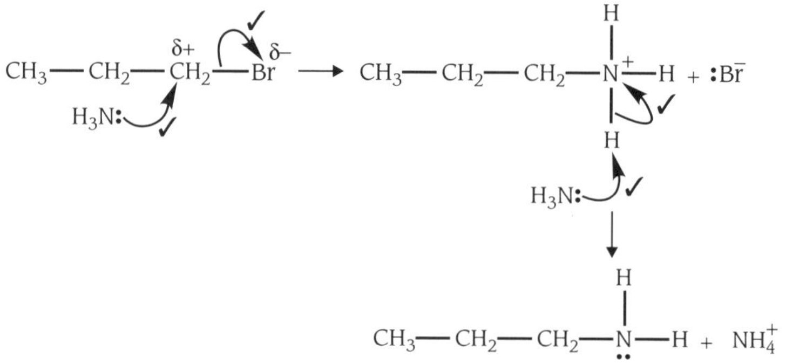

Provided the structures are correct, the four curly arrows score the 4 marks. The first curly arrow is only correct if the lone pair is shown on the ammonia. The second curly arrow must start at the bond and finish at the bromine atom. The third curly arrow is only correct if there is a positive charge on the nitrogen. The fourth curly arrow is only correct if a lone pair is shown on the ammonia.

(b) The haloalkane is $BrCH_2CH_2CH_2CH_2CH_2CH_2Br$ ✓.
$Br(CH_2)_6Br + 4NH_3 \longrightarrow H_2N(CH_2)_6NH_2 + 2NH_4Br$ ✓✓

This is a difficult question. To produce an amine, a bromine atom is substituted by an NH_2 group from ammonia. To produce a diamine, two bromine atoms are substituted, requiring two ammonia molecules. Many candidates can identify the haloalkane but find the equation difficult. The simplified equation, using two NH_3 molecules and producing two HBr molecules, would score 1 mark.

(c) (i) Compound P: $CH_3CH{=}CHCH_3$ ✓; but-2-ene ✓
Compound Q: $CH_3CHBrCH_2CH_3$ ✓; 2-bromobutane ✓
Compound R: $CH_3CH(OH)CH_2CH_3$ ✓; butan-2-ol ✓
Compound S: $CH_3CH(CN)CH_2CH_3$ ✓; 2-methylbutanenitrile ✓
Compound T: $CH_3CH(COOH)CH_2CH_3$ ✓; 2-methylbutanoic acid ✓
The structural formula for 2-methylbutanoic acid is usually written as $CH_3CH_2CH(CH_3)COOH$.

Provided you realise that the original alkene can only be but-2-ene, identifying the structures is straightforward. If you identify the alkene as but-1-ene, you could still score 4 marks for the remaining correct structures. If you identify the alkene as methylpropene, all the structures will be incorrect. However, the examiner will try to give you credit if you have given some correct chemistry. You will be given credit for replacing Br with OH and CN, provided that the consequential structures are correct. The naming of compounds P, Q and R is relatively straightforward. Only the most able candidates will be able to name S and T. In all the names, it is essential that the number 2 is included to show the position of the functional group or side chain. A common mistake is to name compound T as 3-methylbutanoic acid. Remember, the carboxylic acid group is always number 1, so the methyl group is in the 2 position on the chain.

(ii) The mechanism for conversion of P to Q is electrophilic addition ✓. The mechanism for Q to R is nucleophilic substitution ✓.

The question asks you to state the mechanisms so there are no alternative answers. **Hydrolysis** would be acceptable as a reaction *type* but not as a reaction *mechanism*.

(iii) The mechanism for the conversion of Q to S is shown below.

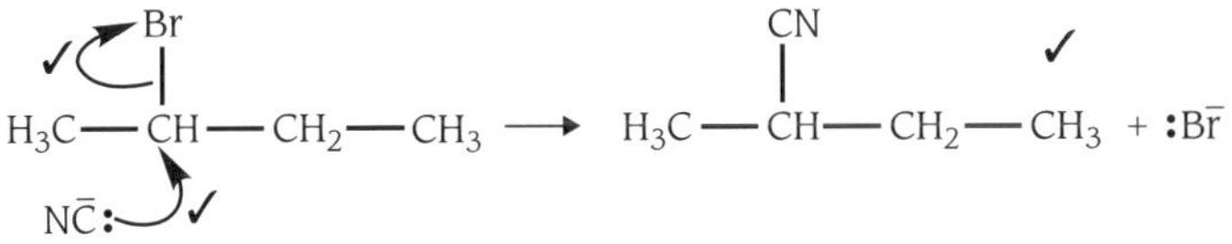

There are 3 marks for the mechanism. 1 mark is scored if the lone pair and the negative charge are shown on the cyanide ion and the curly arrow is in the correct position. There is 1 mark for the curly arrow from the bond to the bromine atom and 1 mark for the correct products.

(d) The structures of compounds A to D are shown below.

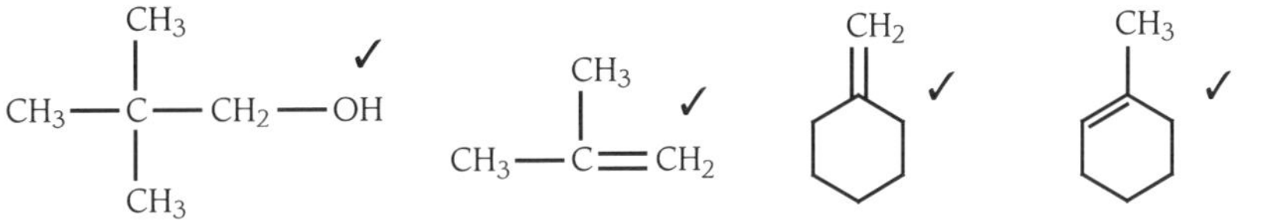

Compound A Compound B Compound C Compound D

The key to this question is remembering that when the solvent is aqueous, substitution takes place and the Br atom is replaced by the OH group. If the solvent is alcoholic, then elimination takes place — the Br atom is lost and a hydrogen atom is lost from the neighbouring carbon atom. In the final part, it is possible for hydrogen to be lost from different adjacent carbon atoms, labelled a or b below, leading to the formation of two different products. Compounds C and D can be interchanged.

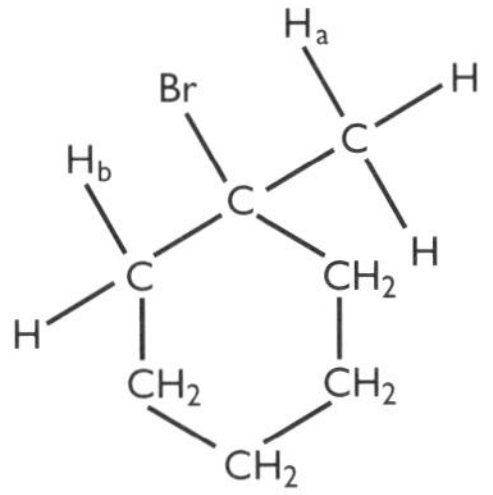

Alcohols

(5) (a) The formula C_3H_8O represents two isomeric alcohols, A and B. Use the information on the flow chart to answer the questions below.

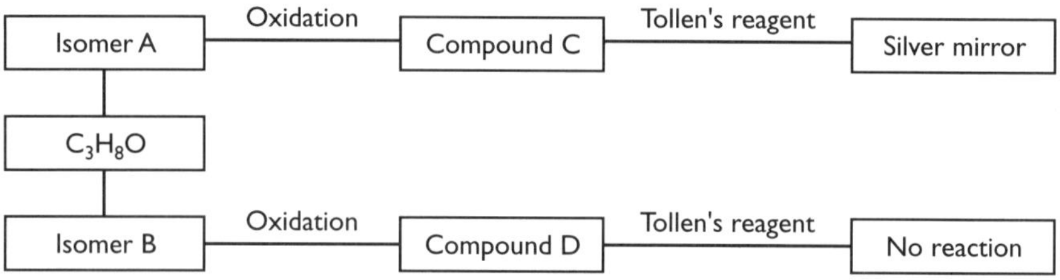

(i) **Give the structural formulae and names of A, B, C and D.** (8 marks)

(ii) **State the reagents and conditions used for the conversion of isomer A into compound C.** (2 marks)

(iii) **State the formula of the organic compound produced when compound C reacts with Tollen's reagent.** (1 mark)

(b) Prop-2-en-1-ol, $CH_2{=}CHCH_2OH$, shows the properties of both an alkene and a primary alcohol.

(i) **Give the structure of the product formed when prop-2-en-1-ol is treated with acidified potassium dichromate and the product is immediately distilled off as it forms.** (1 mark)

(ii) **Give the structure of the product formed when prop-2-en-1-ol is treated with acidified potassium dichromate and the reactants are refluxed.** (1 mark)

(iii) **State the type of reaction and give the structure of the product obtained when prop-2-en-1-ol is treated with bromine in an organic solvent.** (2 marks)

(iv) **Write equations for the reduction of the product in (i), when it is treated with:**

- **hydrogen in the presence of a nickel catalyst**
- **$NaBH_4$ in methanol** (4 marks)

(c) Ethanol can be manufactured industrially by two different methods.
Method 1: ethene reacts directly with steam to produce ethanol in the presence of a concentrated phosphoric acid catalyst at 300 °C and 6.5 MPa.
Method 2: grain is used as a raw material — it requires the presence of yeast and a temperature of about 35 °C.

(i) **Give an equation for, and classify the type of, the reaction taking place in method 1.** (2 marks)

(ii) **State the process involved, name the compound that is converted to ethanol and give an equation to describe the process occurring in method 2.** (4 marks)

(iii) **Give *one* advantage and *one* disadvantage of the grain-based process for the production of ethanol compared with that using ethene.** (2 marks)

(d) Predict the structures of the organic compounds produced when butan-1-ol, propan-2-ol and cyclohexanol are dehydrated with concentrated sulphuric acid. (3 marks)

Total: 30 marks

■ ■ ■

Grade-A answer to Question 5

(a) (i) A = $CH_3CH_2CH_2OH$ ✓; propan-1-ol ✓
B = $CH_3CH(OH)CH_3$ ✓; propan-2-ol ✓
C = CH_3CH_2CHO ✓; propanal ✓
D = CH_3COCH_3 ✓; propanone ✓

e The key to identifying alcohols and carbonyls is the silver mirror test. Only aldehydes give a positive result with Tollen's reagent and they are formed by the oxidation of primary alcohols. Isomer B is a secondary alcohol; its oxidation produces a ketone.

(ii) Acidified $K_2Cr_2O_7$ ✓; distillation ✓

e Either **acidified** or **with dilute H_2SO_4** must be included. **Acidified $KMnO_4$** is an alternative answer.

(iii) CH_3CH_2COOH ✓

e In this reaction, the aldehyde is oxidised further to a carboxylic acid. It takes place in alkaline conditions, so **$CH_3CH_2COO^-$** is an acceptable structure.

(b) (i) CH_2=CH–CHO ✓

e A primary alcohol produces an aldehyde in distillation conditions.

(ii) CH_2=CH–COOH ✓

e A primary alcohol produces a carboxylic acid under reflux.

(iii) Electrophilic addition ✓; $CH_2BrCHBrCH_2OH$ ✓

e Bromine attacks the electron-rich double bond, which is susceptible to electrophilic attack. Bromine does not attack the double bond in the carbonyl group, because carbonyl groups are attacked by nucleophilic reagents.

(iv) $CH_2=CH\text{–}CHO + 2H_2 \longrightarrow CH_3CH_2CH_2OH$ ✓✓
$CH_2=CH\text{–}CHO + 2[H] \longrightarrow CH_2=CH\text{–}CH_2OH$ ✓✓

e Hydrogen reduces both the carbonyl (C=O) group and the alkene (C=C) group, whereas $NaBH_4$ is a more selective reducing agent, only reducing the carbonyl group.

(c) (i) $CH_2=CH_2 + H_2O \longrightarrow CH_3CH_2OH$ ✓
The reaction is a hydration ✓.

e The structure of the alcohol must be given. $C_2H_4 + H_2O \longrightarrow C_2H_5OH$ is acceptable, but $C_2H_4 + H_2O \longrightarrow C_2H_6O$ is not acceptable.

(ii) The process is fermentation ✓. Glucose ✓ is converted to ethanol.
$C_6H_{12}O_6 \longrightarrow 2C_2H_5OH + 2CO_2$ ✓✓

In the equation, there is 1 mark for the products and 1 mark for balancing the equation.

(iii) An advantage of this process is that it uses a renewable resource ✓. A disadvantage is that it gives a lower yield than the hydration process ✓.

Another advantage is that **fuel costs are lower**. Other disadvantages are that **the rate of production is slow** and **it is a batch process, so is more expensive**.

(d) Dehydration of butan-1-ol produces $CH_3CH_2CH{=}CH_2$ ✓. Propan-2-ol is reduced to $CH_3CH{=}CH_2$ ✓. Cyclohexanol is reduced to the structure below.

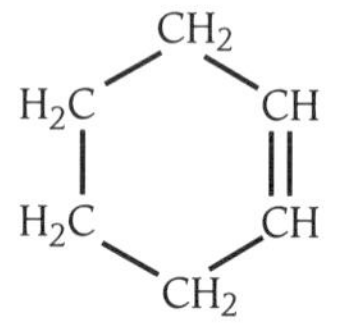

You need to remember how to predict the structure of the alkene from the alcohol — remove the OH group from the alcohol and another H atom from the adjacent carbon atom. In some alcohols, it is possible to remove an H atom from either side of the carbon bearing the OH group, leading to two different alkenes. In addition, some of the alkenes produced could exhibit geometrical isomerism.